Due Process and Higher Education
A Systemic Approach to Fair Decision Making

Ed Stevens

ASHE-ERIC Higher Education Report Volume 27, Number 2

Prepared by

ERIC Clearinghouse on Higher Education
The George Washington University
URL: www.eriche.org

In cooperation with

ASHE

Association for the Study
of Higher Education
URL: http://www.tiger.coe.missouri.edu/~ashe

Published by

Graduate School of Education and Human Development
The George Washington University
URL: www.gwu.edu

Adrianna J. Kezar, Series Editor

Cite as
Stevens, E. (1999). *Due process and higher education: A systemic approach to fair decision making.* ASHE-ERIC Higher Education Report (Vol. 27, No. 2). Washington, DC: The George Washington University, Graduate School of Education and Human Development.

Library of Congress Catalog Card Number 99-64065
ISSN 0884-0040
ISBN 1-878380-90-7

Managing Editor: Lynne J. Scott
Manuscript Editor: Barbara M. Fishel
Cover Design by Michael David Brown, Inc., The Red Door
  Gallery, Rockport, ME

The ERIC Clearinghouse on Higher Education invites individuals to submit proposals for writing monographs for the *ASHE-ERIC Higher Education Report* series. Proposals must include:
1. A detailed manuscript proposal of not more than five pages.
2. A chapter-by-chapter outline.
3. A 75-word summary to be used by several review committees for the initial screening and rating of each proposal.
4. A vita and a writing sample.

ERIC Clearinghouse on Higher Education
Graduate School of Education and Human Development
The George Washington University
One Dupont Circle, Suite 630
Washington, DC 20036-1183

The mission of the ERIC system is to improve American education by increasing and facilitating the use of educational research and information on practice in the activities of learning, teaching, educational decision making, and research, wherever and whenever these activities take place.

This publication was prepared partially with funding from the Office of Educational Research and Improvement, U.S. Department of Education, under contract no. ED-99-00-0036. The opinions expressed in this report do not necessarily reflect the positions or policies of OERI or the Department.

EXECUTIVE SUMMARY

Justice and due process are inseparable. When facts are in dispute, the ideal of just decision making requires unbiased, principled deliberation. Simultaneously, the constitutional concept of due process demands fundamental fairness in the method by which discretionary power is exercised. In higher education, a link between due process and discretionary justice is crucial. University officials and faculty at all ranks are frequently required to make discretionary decisions based on interpretations of disputed facts. By applying the concept of due process in the context of higher education, they can meet the legal challenges of contract and constitutional law and the pedagogical demand for justice.

To guide their efforts to comply with the requirements of due process, decision makers in higher education can turn to a body of case law that has evolved over the last half century. These cases, which address criminal procedure, administrative law, and a range of constitutional issues, underlie an approach to fair, or "systemic," decision making, which can be used as a guide in the principled resolution of disputed facts in the academic setting. Approaching disputes from the perspective of due process not only protects educational professionals from legal liability, but also provides a method whereby the resolution of disputes can serve pedagogical and therapeutic purposes.

The concept of due process has come to embody the essence of fair decision making in criminal, civil, and administrative law. Due process generally requires adequate notice and a meaningful opportunity to be heard, but these requirements involve intertwined substantive and procedural considerations. A systemic approach to the provision of due process in higher education ensures fair decision making in higher education.

What Is Due Process? When Are Due Process Procedures Required?

The phrase "due process" is found in the Fifth and Fourteenth Amendments to the U. S. Constitution, which require that the federal and state governments (respectively) provide citizens with substantive fairness and certain procedures or "process" before depriving them of life, liberty, or property interests. In an extreme case, when a government prosecutor proposes to take a citizen's life as punishment for a crime, that citizen is due, for example, an attorney, a trial before an unbiased judge, and an automatic appeal to the Supreme Court.

Similarly, when a state government, acting through its publicly funded university, proposes to punish a medical student for misconduct by taking from her the opportunity to continue to study at the school, the school must first notify the student of its intentions and provide a hearing in accordance with procedures appropriate to the deprivation. The courts have intentionally retained flexibility in the interpretation of the requirements of due process in higher education, and no exact formula exists for the process due in any individual situation.

What Are the Expectations of the Courts With Regard to Due Process in Higher Education?

The courts have granted tremendous deference to the decisions of administrators and professors in higher education. Before the 1960s, it was extremely rare for a court to even consider the propriety or fairness of a college's academic evaluation or disciplinary action (Wright, 1969). Schools were said to stand in loco parentis with respect to their students and assumed to act in their best interests. That broad discretionary authority has diminished considerably in recent decades. Modern courts require that university policies and regulations not infringe upon the established constitutional rights of professors or students. If a school decides to deprive a student or employee of a constitutionally protected interest, it must provide notice and a hearing commensurate with the interest at stake. The courts continue to allow institutions of higher education considerable discretion in deciding how due process protection shall be provided, and interfere with academic and disciplinary decisions only when constitutional standards are clearly violated.

How Do Legal Requirements for Fair Decision Making Differ in Publicly Supported and Private Institutions?

The Fourteenth Amendment requires a publicly funded university, as an arm of the state government, to provide due process before depriving an individual of protected liberty or property interests. Under contract law, a private college may be held to this same standard if it promises in official literature to provide due process in connection with disciplinary action against members of the institutional community. Both public and private schools are legally obligated to fairly and reasonably carry out the requirements of their written and implied contracts with students and faculty. These contractual duties may parallel the requirements of constitutional due process, depending on the legal interpretation of the wording of the documents that create the contracts.

How Does the Systemic Approach to Due Process Differ From Other Methods of Providing Due Process in Higher Education?

A number of recent publications have promulgated model student codes (Pavela, 1990; Stoner & Cerminara, 1990), model hearing procedures (Bienstock, 1996), and other systems for complying with the demands of administrative and constitutional law in higher education. But no single code or procedural model can anticipate and address the countless variations in circumstances likely to arise. The systemic approach relies less on specificity in regulations and consistency in hearing procedures and more on an understanding, throughout the institution, of the principle of due process.

Those involved in official proceedings tend to evaluate procedural justice on the basis of perceived neutrality; fairness appears to be defined in terms of perceived bias, honesty, and fact-based decision making (Lind et al., 1990). But participation, dignity, and trust could be more important determinants of judgments about the fairness of judicial proceedings. Based on a growing body of research in "therapeutic jurisprudence," it can be said that when people have the opportunity to actively participate in hearings where they are treated with dignity and respect, they tend to have greater trust in those who conduct the hearings and are more receptive to the decisions rendered (Wexler & Winick, 1996). This principle has important implications for due process hearings in higher education.

Due process is not a single event that occurs in isolation. A university should promote system-wide respect for the principles of due process by ensuring that all official inquiries into disputed facts are conducted in a predictable and dignified manner, that any members of the institutional community who face official action adverse to their protected interests receive proper notice and a meaningful opportunity to present and respond to evidence, and that academic and disciplinary decisions are made by unbiased officials. Compliance with the essential principles of due process in the context of higher education will reduce institutional and personal liability, and will lead to fair and just outcomes.

CONTENTS

FOREWORD

Legal issues have become more and more prevalent on college campuses over the last 20 years. A recent ASHE-ERIC monograph, *The Academic Administrator and the Law: What Every Dean and Department Chair Needs to Know,* by Doug Toma and Richard Palm has become one of our top-selling monographs. As noted in the foreword of that volume, higher education was once sheltered from the onslaught of lawsuits that have become common in other sectors, but the tide has turned. Unfortunately, resource materials or guides for colleges and universities to address legal issues are lacking. Over the last 10 years, the National Association of College and University Attorneys (started in 1961) has grown substantially to support the need for additional professionals and to create an understanding of legal issues particular to higher education. Higher education has no choice but to develop careful and sound policies for addressing legal issues, including for ensuring due process.

Because of the litany of new legal issues, due process has become an important principle for presidents, deans, department chairs, and professors. Each group is involved in decisions where discretionary power must be exercised based on disputed facts. Decisions involving due process are made all the time, yet in this litigious time in our country, it is extremely important that this process be applied correctly. Mistakes can be extremely costly for the institution. Every week the *Chronicle of Higher Education* highlights a case of staff, faculty, or student whose rights were violated and received a large in- or out-of-court settlement from a college campus. Legal issues can no longer be left to university counsel; all decision-making members of the academic community must be informed.

The major issues involving due process relate to dismissals of students from campus, firings of staff members, and tenure and promotion for faculty. Moreover, new issues are emerging related to decisions about dismissal, firing, and tenure, such as sexual harassment, discrimination, and substance abuse. As issues change, new policies need to be developed, communicated, and followed. And recent Supreme Court cases are changing the legal landscape once again. In *Davis v. Monroe County,* for example, the Supreme Court established that institutions are liable for failing to stop student-on-student sexual harassment. Specific elements of due process that relate to sexual harassment might differ from substance abuse cases. To clarify the expectations of campuses and due process procedures, many campuses are developing statements of students' rights and responsibilities or faculty codes. Such documents are not new on campus, but they are being embraced more broadly. In addition, many campuses' codes or statements were not previously enforced, but there now exists a greater effort to inform the community of both rights and responsibilities. Due process is an important part of individuals' rights that they must be informed about.

Ed Stevens, associate professor and chair of the Department of Criminal Justice and Social Sciences at Troy State University, wrote *Due Process and Higher Education: A Systemic Approach to Fair Decision Making* to address the dearth of resources on due process in higher education. It is assuredly a significant contribution to the literature. Because this territory is new for many administrators in higher education, Stevens reviews a definition of this concept and describes its evolution as a legal principle. He provides a detailed analysis of how due process is handled within the context of higher education, examining differences within sectors. Last, he presents a new systemic framework for ensuring accurate execution. The case studies in the appendixes and on the ERIC website *(www.eriche.org/reports/scenarios.html)* provide a mechanism for teaching others about due process and help individuals to better understand implementation of due process.

Other monographs in the ASHE-ERIC Series may be of interest to readers. *Reconciling Rights and Responsibilities of Colleges and Students* by Annette Gibbs helps to shed light on key issues such as free speech on campus, the right of assembly, the rights of student organizations, and mandatory drug testing. *Academic Freedom in American Higher Education* by Robert Poch reviews this concept historically and within the current context; with tenure processes being reevaluated on many college campuses, this monograph is timely in its presentation of information on policy. *Tenure, Promotion, and Reappointment* by Benjamin Baez and John Centra also focuses on the legal issues surrounding the tenure process and covers issues such as contractual rights, discrimination, and affirmative action. Last, *Sexual Harassment in Higher Education* by Robert Riggs, Patricia Murrell, and JoAnne Cutting presents the legal bases and origins of sexual harassment and institutional responses. These monographs examine in detail all the key legal issues affecting higher education and offer practical solutions for addressing them. Build your collection of resources and begin training your staff now. The longer your campus waits, the greater your chance of liability.

Adrianna J. Kezar
Series Editor,
Assistant Professor of Higher Education, and
Director, ERIC Clearinghouse on Higher Education

INTRODUCTION

*Where law ends, tyranny need not begin. Where law
ends, discretion begins, and the exercise of discretion
may mean either beneficence or tyranny, either justice
or injustice, either reasonableness or arbitrariness.*
(Davis, 1969, p. 3)

The key concept in most litigation pitting American institutions of higher education against students, faculty, or other
employees is the ideal of "due process." Because colleges
and universities can wield enormous direct and indirect
influence over the lives of those they employ and educate,
justification exists in the field of higher education for the
application of principles that can temper the potential for
abuse of discretionary power. Due process implies fairness
in the substance of the rules that govern and rationality in
the procedures by which decisions are made.

The Due Process Clause of the Fourteenth Amendment to
the U. S. Constitution has been interpreted to require that
before a state government may deprive a citizen of life or
certain liberty and property interests, the citizen must be
provided with appropriate notice and a meaningful opportunity to dispute the basis for that sanction. As an accused
criminal is entitled to an adversarial trial before the imposition of punishment, before a state university may deprive a
student or a professor of constitutionally protected interests,
the accused is entitled to the essence of substantive and
procedural due process: a fair hearing. A similar fairness
requirement applying to private schools may arise under
tenets of contract law. Legally, and perhaps morally, it can
be said that before exercising its discretion to decide matters
of disputed fact, an institution of higher education, public or
private, should be guided by the principle of due process.

Over the past several decades, American courts have ex-
perienced an explosion in the number of lawsuits filed to re-
dress an array of manifest grievances and perceived injustices.
Institutions of higher education have not escaped the impact

of this explosion in litigation. As educational degrees become gateways to economic advancement and tuition costs spiral, students and professors are more inclined to view their relationships to higher education in legal and specifically contractual terms. It is therefore not surprising to see increased litigation involving colleges and universities. More students challenge academic and disciplinary decisions in the courtroom, more professors file lawsuits over issues involving promotion and tenure, and heretofore unknown grounds for legal action are rapidly developing. The legislative branches of the federal and state governments have greatly expanded the opportunities for plaintiffs to sue in response to discrimination based on gender and disability. The courts have embraced these and other causes of action that were unknown only a few decades ago. Although colleges and universities still win more cases than they lose, the explosion in litigation can be expected to continue and institutions of higher education must be prepared for increased judicial scrutiny.

A university may face legal action based not only on the position it takes in a matter of disputed facts, but also on how it arrives at that position. As professionals and administrators in institutions of higher education face the challenges involved in properly deciding disputes with their employees and students, they can find guidance in a line of U. S. Supreme Court cases that describe due process in terms of the proper relationship between American citizens and their government. By understanding the process that state governments are required by the Fourteenth Amendment to provide, public as well as private school administrators can discern a method for fair inquiry that is appropriate in relation to their inherent discretionary power. It remains for those administrators to apply the principles of due process in good faith. When they do so, they not only uphold the ideal of fundamental fairness but also provide their schools with defenses to unwarranted litigation.

One of the hallmarks of a democratic society is the ability of an aggrieved citizen to legally challenge unfair or wrongful conduct, but society pays a price when it encourages broad access to the courts. Litigation, especially civil litigation, can be an expensive, disquieting, and agonizingly slow process. An individual's life can be devastated, not only by a finding of liability in a lawsuit alleging such conduct as discrimination or sexual harassment, but also simply by filing such a case. A campus can be torn apart by even the threat of litigation. In the wake of such a threat, reputations and careers can be irreparably damaged, and the sense of a university community, built over decades or centuries, can be suddenly injured or destroyed.

The fear of litigation has tempted administrators at some institutions of higher education to spend unjustified amounts of money, to award unjustified grades, and even to modify long-standing academic requirements. A major source of this fear stems from uncertainty as to the requirements of the law, especially the responsibilities generated by the Fourteenth Amendment. Many professors and administrators at public institutions of higher education realize that the Fourteenth Amendment requires due process before the deprivation of property or liberty interests, but they are confused about the practical steps that are therefore necessary. Similar problems may arise for administrators at private educational institutions who know that actual or implied contracts between schools and students require that they proceed in a manner that the law deems fair and reasonable, but find those terms uncomfortably vague when applied in real-life situations. Confusion over due process and contractual requirements is further complicated by the myriad of laws, policies, regulations, and apparently conflicting court decisions that form the body of law governing higher education. Literally thousands of decisions apply due process standards in specific educational situations, and "one can find cases on both sides of almost every specific question of what process need be afforded" (Hustoles & Duerr, 1994, p. 2). Although such uncertainty in the law is disturbing for those who must make decisions, it also illustrates the flexibility of the due process standard and the fact that courts examine each case on its own merits when determining what procedural safeguards are due.

A number of authors have recently addressed the need for practical guidance in responding to disputes in higher education (Bienstock, 1996; Cole, 1994; Hollander, Young, & Gehring, 1995; Stoner & Cerminara, 1990). Others delve into the fine points of specific issues in higher education that commonly result in legal challenges, such as disputes about tenure (Baez & Centra, 1995), discrimination with regard to race and disability (Hustoles & Connolly, 1990; Kaufman, 1991; Rothstein, 1991), and sexual harassment (Cole, 1990). The intent of this report is to provide practical information

The fear of litigation has tempted administrators at some institutions of higher education to spend unjustified amounts of money . . .

that educators and administrators can use as they strive to make fair decisions and comply with the law. Toward that end, the constitutional and contractual requirements for due process are examined in various kinds of cases that arise in higher education, and a method is proposed by which fair decision making may be obtained at all levels (from the classroom to the committee meeting to the president's office) within a university setting.

This report explores several themes. The first is that due process is a flexible and evolving standard that can be meaningfully applied in the context of higher education cases. Due process is a broad touchstone for fairness and legitimacy. Without violating this concept, the same case could be addressed by different universities in different ways. As the courts examine the application of due process in higher education, the inquiry involves fairness in the totality of the circumstances, rather than strict compliance with rigid procedural rules. Conceptualized as a principle of fairness, due process becomes more than a constitutional requirement: It can also provide a technique for resolving disputes and, in institutional management, a method for meeting the constitutional and contractual demands the law places on relationships involving students, faculty, employees, and colleges.

A second theme of this report is that the courts, primarily the U. S. Supreme Court over the past 30 years, have articulated a workable and accessible due process scheme that can be used for fair decision making in the specific context of higher education. This broad scope of the Supreme Court's conceptual scheme defies a complete quantitative description, but its philosophy can be expressed and its components can be set out. The principle of due process demands that an opportunity for a meaningful hearing be offered to those who will be affected by official decisions and that the hearing be conducted in a sensible and dignified manner. Further, due process requires that the ultimate decision reached by an institution of higher education be trustworthy, not an arbitrary exercise of the school's discretionary power. These attributes of due process imply an inquiry based on an open-minded, good faith examination of both sides of disputed facts, respect for the rights of the parties involved, and a principled decision that is based specifically on the information and facts elicited during the inquiry.

This report describes a systemic approach to due process in higher education based on the literature and legal cases addressing this crucial constitutional concept. The components of this approach include, first, attention to substantive concerns to prevent the ultimate decision from being arbitrary and capricious. These substantive concerns include proper notice to students and employees of the rules and regulations by which they are expected to abide, the assurance that in each specific case those regulations will operate reasonably and fairly, and safeguards against institutional bias.

The second part of the systemic approach described here addresses the procedural aspect of due process. To assure that the case proceeds in accordance with the principles of due process, an administrator in higher education begins with an analysis of the nature of the case to decide the appropriate level of overall procedural complexity. Some cases involve facts in such dispute and consequences so serious that trial-like methods and adversarial proceedings are required. In other cases, less procedural complexity is justified, and methods for hearing the facts can be less formal. For example, disciplinary cases involving students generally require far more due process protection than inquiries into a student's academic competence. Although a student who challenges a professor's evaluation may be entitled to an informal hearing, the courts very rarely disturb a university's assessment of a student's academic competence. On the other hand, the consequences involved in a dispute over an alleged sexual assault by one student against another are so serious that a university hearing that resembles a trial may be necessary before the imposition of discipline. The judgment as to the appropriate level of procedural complexity required in a given case is the first of many discretionary decisions that must be made with respect to the procedure that will be observed at the hearing.

The second step toward procedural due process involves the selection of an appropriate, unbiased decision maker for the case at hand. Depending on the seriousness of the case and the potential bias involved, decisions in a case may be made by a classroom professor, a department chair or dean, an established or ad hoc committee, an institutional administrator, or, in rare cases, by someone from outside the university community. At some schools, existing regulations specify who must decide certain types of cases; these regulations should always be strictly observed. More often, however, the mechanics of due process are left to the discretion of educational administrators, who must guard against institutional or personal bias as facts are explored and decisions rendered.

The remaining step toward obtaining procedural due process can be divided into three parts: (a) the provision of safeguards to ensure proper notice; (b) procedures to provide a fair hearing; and (c) for purposes of truly systemic due process, safeguards that provide access to a meaningful appeal mechanism. In other words, the final consideration in seeking procedural due process involves decisions about appropriate procedural safeguards before, during, and after the hearing in each case.

Strong reasons exist for colleges and universities to incorporate a rigorous due process standard in all official inquiries and practices. As indicated, due process claims are a part of most litigation involving institutions of higher education. Good faith adherence to the requirements of this constitutional principle can effectively shield not only the university from unjustified legal action, but also individual administrators and professors as they undertake the crucial academic and disciplinary decisions that are the essence of their employment. By implementing institution-wide, or *systemic,* policies based on an application of constitutional due process principles as a method of inquiry, universities create defenses against unwarranted litigation. In short, although due process is the legal sword with which unfair institutional conduct may be attacked, it is also a potential shield against unfair legal action.

When professors, department chairs, deans, and other administrators in higher education use due process as the touchstone for resolution of academic disputes, they also have the opportunity to facilitate what has been called "therapeutic jurisprudence" (Wexler & Winick, 1991). This perspective examines the effects of participation in the legal or quasi-legal process and suggests that such participation, quite apart from the decision rendered, has a powerful effect. "People are affected by the way in which decisions are made, irrespective of what those decisions are" (Tyler, 1996, p. 7). The closing theme of this report is that due process, by providing the opportunity for meaningful participation in a dignified proceeding, engenders an outcome that the parties can more easily perceive as trustworthy and just. These attributes (participation, dignity, and trust) can increase individual and collective receptivity to decisions rendered in higher education. This outcome may be equally as important as conforming those decisions to the requirements of constitutional and contract law.

Without question, modern courts will reverse educational decisions that clearly violate constitutional rights. Even decisions based on academic expertise cannot withstand judicial scrutiny when shown to be motivated by ill will or bad faith unrelated to academic performance (Cole, 1994). In a line of cases requiring that due process be afforded by state-supported institutions, the Supreme Court responded to the need for practical guidance in the resolution of disputes that arise on campus. The Court set out a philosophy based on the fair selection of adaptable due process procedures and thus articulated a method by which a myriad of difficult educational decisions may be made. Rather than viewing the requirement of due process as a barrier or a lawyer's trap, professionals at all levels of higher education can share in the development of systemic methods for fair decision making that not only protect institutions from legal liability, but also actually lead to justice and the opportunity for greater institutional and personal integrity.

After describing the academic and historical development of due process in the context of higher education in America and some of the fundamental concepts involved in the application of due process, this report offers an approach to the implementation of this constitutional ideal. It presents a systemic method for operationalizing substantive and procedural due process, describing various procedural safeguards that may be appropriate in hearings conducted by colleges and universities. The report concludes with brief observations concerning the psychological consequences of participation in official hearings and speculation on how justice and even therapeutic outcomes may result from the implementation of systemic due process in institutions of higher education.

AN OVERVIEW OF DUE PROCESS
IN HIGHER EDUCATION

The Literature on Due Process

The literature addressing the subject of due process of law and its relationship to higher education can be divided into several distinct categories. The first of these categories involves literature concerned with the development of the concept of due process from historical, theoretical, and academic perspectives. A second category could be labeled "law-related" or "case-related" literature, including the legal cases themselves and law review articles and journals that analyze administrative and criminal law. The audience for this substantial body of work has been the legal community. Recently, efforts have been made to make this attorney-oriented literature more accessible to those not trained in the law. This practical, general information on the legal and constitutional requirements applicable to institutions of higher education, and especially the requirements of due process, constitutes a third category of the relevant literature.

Academic perspectives

To apply the principles of due process in specific situations in higher education, one must possess some understanding of the historical development of limitations on sovereign authority. A number of erudite and scholarly works trace this concept back to its early English origins and reflect on the philosophy of governance that due process embodies. For purposes of American higher education, perhaps the finest overall collection of essays in this category is contained in a book in a series published by the American Society for Political and Legal Philosophy, *Due Process* (Pennock & Chapman, 1977). Several of the essays in the book directly address, or use case examples involving, due process in higher education. Other important works in the general category of scholarly essays include those by Bailyn (1967), Haines (1930), Perelman (1967), and Rawls (1971).

Encompassed in the broad category of general background information on due process as it affects higher education are works addressing specific topics such as sexual harassment, discrimination based on disability, tenure, and dismissal. Cases involving these topics may or may not raise procedural due process issues, depending on the facts in the case. For example, as described in more depth later, cases in which a professor is denied tenure after undergoing a fair and comprehensive review or a professor without tenure is not rehired after her contract expires may not involve issues of procedural due process. But when those decisions are based, even in part, on choices between differing versions of the relevant facts, an inquiry into those facts, in accordance with the principles of due process, becomes critical. In such cases, it is necessary for those exercising professional discretion to understand the substantive elements involved in specific legal topics. The rapidly developing law regarding sexual harassment in the workplace, and new statutory protection against discrimination, for example, involve traditional due process principles in specific contexts. Among the references at the conclusion of this report are sources describing legal issues that frequently become the subject of due process hearings in higher education.

Case-related literature

A second category of literature addressing due process and higher education began to emerge during the 1960s in response to the civil rights movement and a number of cases involving students' rights of the time. A groundbreaking case, *Dixon v. Alabama State Board of Education* (1961), awakened the courts to the existence of constitutional rights on college campuses. In response, a number of legal scholars  began to explore issues involving due process and institutions of higher education in law reviews and legal journals. The best examples of these types of articles include "The Constitution on the Campus" (Wright, 1969) and "The Student as University Resident" (Van Alstyne, 1968). Although these articles are somewhat dated, they provide useful background information on the application of due process in the field of higher education.

Over the decades since *Dixon*, the U.S. Supreme Court has announced or clarified the due process rights of university professors and students on several occasions. In the early 1970s in *Board of Regents of State Colleges v. Roth* (1972), the Court held that unless a nontenured university professor could demonstrate that he had constitutionally protected interests in addition to his one-year contract, he had no right to a hearing before the decision not to renew that contract. In a companion case, *Perry v. Sindermann* (1972), however, the Court ruled that a professor in a university system without a formal tenure policy could rely on an informal understanding regarding continued employment, and that this expectation could create a property right protected by due process.

In the mid-1970s, the Court clarified the requirements of minimal due process for the discipline of students in *Goss v. Lopez* (1975) and the scope of school officials' "qualified good faith immunity" from legal liability for the violation of students' civil rights in *Wood v. Strickland* (1975). Later in that decade, the Court reversed its trend and began to circumscribe students' due process rights in higher education cases. In *Board of Curators of the University of Missouri v. Horowitz* (1978), the Court refused to enlarge the role of the judiciary in the academic community, holding that a student dismissed from medical school for academic reasons was not entitled to a hearing. This position was reaffirmed in *Regents of the University of Michigan v. Ewing* (1985), which did not foreclose all "academic challenges" in higher education but raised a high standard for success in such cases. These decisions generated numerous legal articles, the best of which include "Judicial Intervention in the Student-University Relationship: Due Process and Contract Theories" (Latourette & King, 1988), "'Academic Challenge' Cases: Should Judicial Review Extend to Academic Evaluations of Students?" (Schweitzer, 1992), and "The Contract to Educate: Toward a More Workable Theory of the Student-University Relationship" (Nordin, 1980). Also of note is a fascinating argument for the expansion of the rights of students who face disciplinary charges, written by a lawyer who was himself accused of serious misconduct while a university student, "University Disciplinary Process: What's Fair, What's Due, and What You Don't Get" (Picozzi, 1987).

A subcategory of this case-related or "case-generated" literature includes a number of journals and reports devoted to issues involving law and education. Over the past two decades, information and analysis related to education law have been offered in such journals as *The Journal of Law and Education* and *The Journal of College and University Law*. More specifically, the Higher Education Administration series of College Administration Publications publishes quarterly "Reporters," including "The Student and the Courts" and "The College Administrator and the Courts,"* which provide synopses of the range of legal decisions affecting

*Available from College Administration Publications, Inc., P.O. Box 15898, Asheville, NC 28813-0898.

higher education. These journals and reports are directed toward university attorneys and other lawyers who specialize in education law, as well as toward administrators in higher education.

Another important source of legal information addressing due process and higher education is actual court decisions. While some cases are difficult to comprehend, many U. S. Supreme Court decisions addressing higher education can be read as logical, erudite essays describing specific applications of the requirements of due process. To gain what is later referred to in this report as "constitutional competence," all academicians, particularly administrators in the field of higher education, should be familiar with the landmark due process cases. There is probably no better way to gain this familiarity than by going straight to the source and reading the words of the Supreme Court.

Practical literature

A third category of literature addressing due process and higher education, arguably distinct from the previous categories, is the growing body of work that intends to translate the theoretical, academic, and legal literature into practical information that educational administrators and teachers can use daily. *Tenure, Promotion, and Reappointment: Legal and Administrative Implications* (Baez & Centra, 1995) in the ASHE-ERIC Higher Education Reports series and *Selected Legal Issues Relating to Due Process and Liability in Higher Education* (Cole, 1994) are excellent examples of such literature. Other outstanding works in this category of literature can be found in the Higher Education Administration series, including *The Dismissal of Students With Mental Disorders: Legal Issues, Policy Considerations, and Alternative Responses* (Pavela, 1985), *A Practical Guide to Legal Issues Affecting College Teachers* (Hollander et al., 1995), and *A Guide to Conducting a Hearing in a Higher Education Setting* (Bienstock, 1996).

It is not necessary to comprehend the entire body of literature addressing due process to appreciate and apply the concept. Due process is a flexible concept, with different requirements in different circumstances at different times. Seemingly small details in a case may change a court's view as to precedent cases and applicable rules. It is better to cultivate a broad understanding of the requirements of due process in higher education than to rely on specific cases or immutable procedural regulations.

The Historical Development of Due Process

Much has been written about the importance of due process and the right of citizens to be free from arbitrary or unreasonable governmental action (Dunham, 1965; Howard, 1968; Pennock & Chapman, 1977; Perry, 1964). Due process is a central concept in the American constitutional tradition, an idea that assumes the existence of conflicts between the government and citizens and the resolution of those conflicts through lawful proceedings (Miller, 1977). The first written source of the concept is the Magna Carta, the Great Charter of 1215, by which the British king agreed to grant certain procedural rights to English barons. This grant acknowledged that the king was not all-powerful and resulted in the theoretical and judicial development of the right called "substantive due process" (Miller, 1977).

References to the term "due process of law" are rare in English legal writing (Marshall, 1977). In a classic work, *Second Part of the Institutes of the Laws of England,* Sir Edward Coke extracted the term from the Magna Carta's reference to *per legem terrae* or "the law of the land" (1671, p. 46). Over the past century, however, due process has become a distinctly American concept. As justification for their overthrowing the English crown in the Revolutionary War, the American colonists referred to Lord Coke, to the English common law, and to the Magna Carta. Upon winning independence, the American founding fathers placed due process protection in the Fifth Amendment to the Bill of Rights, setting the stage for the development of the concept by the U. S. Supreme Court (Bailyn, 1967).

The earliest American cases dealing with the Due Process Clause of the Fifth Amendment conceived of the phrase as a limitation on the power of the federal Congress. Rather than arbitrarily taking a citizen's life, liberty, or property, the government's actions are required to bear a strong relationship to the achievement of legitimate governmental interests and to proceed according to the forms that evolved over centuries of English common law (Corwin, 1948). The principles of justice that had developed under the common law were held inviolate, and throughout its history, the Supreme Court has used the right to due process as a limitation on the extent to which the law was allowed to alter the procedures in which those principles were embodied. The legal development of the concept of due process did not begin in earnest until after the Civil War, when the Fourteenth Amendment's Due Process Clause granted citizens protection from *state* governments. The courts ultimately settled upon the position that the Constitution does not guarantee life, liberty, or property to citizens but that those interests may not be abridged without due process (Baez & Centra, 1995).

The Supreme Court headed by Chief Justice Earl Warren is credited with the "due process revolution" of the 1960s and 1970s that gradually applied most of the protections in the Bill of Rights to the enforcement of criminal laws by state governments (Zalman & Siegel, 1997). The Warren Court's concern with civil liberties also led to creative and unprecedented interpretations of due process that allowed judicial intervention in a wide range of disputes that had previously been considered private. The Warren Court refined, some would say re-defined, the method by which the requirements of due process should be measured (Wolfe, 1991).

To determine the scope of due process, the Supreme Court has traditionally looked to three sources that are succinctly identified in *In re Gault* (1967). First, what the Court calls the "settled usages and modes of proceeding" are used as the standard for any governmental procedure by which constitutional rights may be infringed—the customs and expectations established by the people over the centuries. Second, the Court measures the seriousness of the citizen's potential loss in terms of the "fundamental principles of liberty and justice [that] lie at the base of all our civil and political institutions"—the philosophical ideals of equality and freedom underlying the Declaration of Independence and the United States Constitution. And third, the "character and requirements of the circumstances presented in each situation" must be considered (p. 68). Thus, due process refers to a "fundamental" fairness that incorporates, but has not been limited to, most of the protections of the Bill of Rights (Zalman & Siegel, 1997). Thus, the relatively narrow character of due process was transformed by the Warren Court into "a blank check for judicial notions of justice," and the breadth of modern due process, in both criminal and civil cases, is unjustified (Wolfe, 1991, p. 223).

The concept of due process has been held to protect or create a number of controversial "rights" that are not expressly stated in the Constitution. The Court has occasionally used a natural law approach, finding some rights so important that they are protected even if they are not mentioned in the Constitution (Tribe, 1973). Under this approach, the government has been prohibited from interfering with the "right to privacy," which protects, for example, the right to have an abortion or to use contraceptives and other freedoms involving intimate association. The Warren Court's explosive development of due process protection reached its peak in the 1970s in cases such as *Goldberg v. Kelly* (1970) and *Mathews v. Eldridge* (1976). These administrative law cases extended the authority of due process substantively and procedurally. Substantive due process prohibits the government from making completely arbitrary decisions that would result in a citizen's loss of protected liberty or property interests, and it generally requires that the government demonstrate a legitimate reason for its actions.

In addition to the requirements of substantive due process, the government may deprive a citizen of protected liberty or property interests only in accordance with fair *procedures.* In criminal cases, the Supreme Court includes the protections found in the fundamental provisions of the Bill of Rights as part of the procedure it demands from the federal government and in prosecutions by the states (Zalman & Siegel, 1997). But although procedural due process is required, there is no rigid formula for its delivery. Consider, for example, the flexibility found in the Sixth Amendment right to a jury trial. Procedural due process, as required by the Fourteenth Amendment's Due Process Clause, demands that states provide juries in criminal cases, but the U. S. Constitution does not require that jurors be unanimous in their verdict and allows juries to comprise fewer than 12 persons (Klotter & Kanovitz, 1995). The substantive requirement that a jury be provided is subject to different methods of procedural implementation by the states. The Supreme Court, in *In re Gault* (1967), held that juveniles facing charges of delinquency were entitled to considerable due process protection but that it did not include the right to a jury. Due process is a standard that varies in application depending on the nature and circumstances of each case in which it is invoked.

Since the Warren Court's expansive application of the Due Process Clause in the 1970s, the Supreme Court has continued to explore the meaning and relevance of this dynamic concept. Much of this development has come in the field of administrative law, where due process is a primary source for the regulation of administrative agencies. With the rise of the "administrative state" and the increasing rulemaking and adjudicative power in a host of administrative bodies, due process continues to play a crucial role in limiting the power of the federal government.

It can accurately be said that the concept of due process has seen gradual, sustained development since the signing of the Magna Carta in 1215. Due process has become one of the fundamental principles of American law, and it is applied by the courts in a myriad of situations. In each situation, however, the requirements of due process depend on the nature of the interests at stake. The art of applying this flexible standard has very practical consequences in the context of higher education.

Fundamental Concepts of Due Process
The laws by which the American government operates are required by the constitutional principle of substantive due process to be equitable and reasonably clear. Similarly, the procedures used to implement the laws must be rational and appropriate, or a violation of procedural due process may occur. When courts examine university decision making to determine compliance with constitutional standards, requirements for both substantive and procedural due process are considered. To determine the appropriate depth of the procedural safeguards to be employed in any particular case, the courts first look to see whether interests protected by the Due Process Clause of the Fourteenth Amendment are involved. They may be "liberty" or "property" interests, and these terms have distinct legal significance. If the constitutional rights of students or university employees are implicated, the courts then consider the specific facts of each case. When courts address due process claims, they frequently emphasize that the very nature of due process negates any concept of inflexible procedures universally applicable in every imaginable situation. Instead, they hold that, at a minimum, the deprivation of a protected interest must be preceded by notice and an opportunity for a hearing appropriate to the nature of the case (Latourette & King, 1988). This section examines the underlying concepts that enter into this determination.

Substantive due process

Academic or disciplinary decisions that are not based on facts or evidence but are motivated by bad faith, arbitrariness, or capriciousness have traditionally been held to violate substantive due process in higher education (Schweitzer, 1992; see also *Connelly v. University of Vermont* [1995], *Greenhill v. Bailey* [1975], and *Bernard v. Inhabitants of Shelburne* [1913]). A number of recent decisions have augmented this traditional standard, holding that no substantive due process violation exists as long as there is a rational basis for a university's decision (Latourette & King, 1988).

In the context of higher education, substantive due process involves the overall fairness of a school's regulations and policies as well as the fairness of their operation in each particular case. It makes little sense for a university to provide elaborate procedural steps, carefully ensuring that a student is allowed to present his or her case and respond to adverse evidence, without ensuring that the ultimate decision in the case is actually based on the evidence that was presented. If, for example, a university dean or president simply disregards the testimony and evidence elicited at a due process hearing and arbitrarily imposes an unjustified penalty on appeal, then whatever procedural safeguards may have previously been provided become meaningless. Substantive due process requires comprehensive fairness when the case is reviewed in its totality.

To meet the requirement for substantive due process, colleges and universities must continually refine their disciplinary codes and mechanisms in light of evolving constitutional requirements. Optimal university regulations and codes of conduct strike a balance between specificity and flexibility. They clearly specify what kinds of conduct are prohibited and explain what steps will be taken when students or employees engage in prohibited conduct. At the same time, well crafted university policies provide administrators with discretion in how they go about hearing and resolving disputes. Codes of conduct that are too detailed may frustrate attempts to provide the flexibility that allows for the provision of meaningful due process.

An administrator's first duty in the practical application of substantive due process is to comprehend his or her institution's existing scheme for the resolution of disputed facts. The rules that govern the provision of due process may be located in a variety of documents. Student and faculty hand-

Optimal university regulations and codes of conduct strike a balance between specificity and flexibility.

books, college bulletins, official memoranda, and even individual course syllabi may contain binding contractual obligations encompassed by substantive due process. It is the duty of the university administration, in consultation with legal counsel, to create reasonably clear, accessible policies governing the provision of due process, to disseminate this information throughout the institution, and to follow published regulations, even if they go beyond the constitutional requirements of procedural due process.

Most institutions of higher education have relatively well developed policies and regulations governing matters of tenure, misconduct by employees, grievances, and other "professional" issues compared with those describing the due process rights of students. Much of the discussion in this report is therefore devoted to issues of due process for students, which does not mean that the approach described in this report cannot be applied to university employees and faculty members. No code, union contract, or set of regulations could possibly specify the requirements of due process for every possible situation. Because the requirements of due process are flexible, administrators are frequently required to exercise professional discretion with respect to specific procedural safeguards, even when guided by published procedures.

Substantive due process also requires an unbiased decision maker. Whether the ultimate decision in a case is made by an individual or a panel, that decision should rest on the evidence adduced at the hearing rather than on extraneous considerations or preconceived conclusions. In rare cases, the requirement that a school's decision be unbiased may require the involvement of someone from outside the university community.

Procedural due process
The requirement for procedural due process refers to the need for an appropriate hearing format under which fair decisions can be made. While substantive due process requires consideration of the fairness inherent in an entire proceeding, procedural due process involves a range of safeguards, or preventative steps, that are necessary and appropriate to allow the matter to be heard in the depth called for by the nature of the case. Procedural due process, in other words, involves consideration of each discrete step that led to the result in a particular case.

In the context of higher education, courts first look for compliance with the steps prescribed by an institution's existing policy. When an institution, public or private, promises to provide certain safeguards or procedures before taking action against a student or employee, the courts usually require strict compliance. For example, even if the nature of a case is not so serious that constitutional due process would require that a student be provided with legal counsel, when school regulations state that this safeguard will be provided, the courts usually require counsel as a requirement of procedural due process.

Beyond the procedural requirements specified in university regulations, the determination of which specific procedural safeguards are necessary in a given case requires careful consideration of the nature of each case and the range of procedural steps that could be used to obtain a just result. Selecting appropriate procedural safeguards and rejecting unnecessary steps in the process is an art, requiring informed judgment, discretion, and integrity. The words of Justice Felix Frankfurter in *Joint Anti-Fascist Refugee Committee v. McGrath* (1951) are often quoted to emphasize that the nature of due process is "not a mechanical instrument," but "a process." This process may include such safeguards as the right to counsel, the right to a recorded hearing, or the right to a written hearing decision, or it may encompass none of these rights. The exact steps necessary in the process are contingent on the factual situation, the available alternatives, and, as Frankfurter put it, the "balance of the hurt complained of and good accomplished" (p. 163).

Obviously, the concepts of substantive and procedural due process influence and overlap each other. The courts generally regard substantive due process as more important than any specific procedural protection. Thus, even if a school violates its own rules and due process requirements, a court may overlook this problem if it finds that *substantively,* the process provided by the school was appropriate and fair (see *Nash v. Auburn University,* 1987).

Liberty and property interests

As indicated earlier, to determine the extent of the process due, one must consider what is at stake in the particular case or the seriousness of the potential loss. In all but the most serious criminal cases, this determination means the kind of "liberty interest" or "property interest" involved and the seriousness of that interest. These terms have specific meanings in the jurisprudence of due process. A liberty interest protected by the Due Process Clause includes more than being free from physical restraint. Among the various liberty interests the courts have recognized are interests in retaining custody of one's children, in retaining national citizenship, and in retaining one's license to practice a particular profession. More relevant in the context of higher education are protected liberty interests such as engaging in constitutionally protected speech, associating with fellow students or colleagues, seeking employment, and maintaining one's good name and reputation (Rubin & Greenhouse, 1983).

"Property," for purposes of due process, not only includes the money or possessions one has acquired, but also can refer to "entitlements," such as the legal interest in the continuation of welfare or social security benefits, the continuation of utility services supplied by the government, or retention of one's driver's license (Klotter & Kanovitz, 1995). Property interests are not created directly by the U. S. Constitution but must flow from and be defined by an existing rule (as in a school regulation) or an understanding that stems from an independent source such as a state law or a contract. In legal terminology, a protected property interest is said to "attach" to any such understanding. In the setting of higher education, protected property interests have attached to the continuation of a professor's employment by a state university when the professor could demonstrate a legitimate claim based on a contract or on tenure. Students have property interests in the continuation of public education once accepted in a state university. Additionally, the courts find combined liberty and property interests in the continuation of enrollment in public education that will lead to certain professional degrees, such as in medicine or law. This heightened protection explains why many of the leading due process cases in higher education involve students in law school or those pursuing medical degrees.

Institutional tenure regulations, written campus policy statements, contract provisions, and even unwritten mutual understandings can create property interests that are protected by due process. In *Perry v. Sindermann* (1972), the Supreme Court recognized the protected property interest possessed by a nontenured professor who was able to prove that a univer-

Institutional tenure regulations, written campus policy statements, contract provisions, and even unwritten mutual understandings can create property interests that are protected by due process.

sity had an unwritten, but clearly demonstrable, tenure policy that was not followed in his case. The professor was thus entitled to a due process hearing *before* being terminated for his teaching job. In *Board of Regents of State Colleges v. Roth* (1972), however, a professor who had only a 1-year contract and no reasonable expectation that the contract would be renewed was not entitled to a hearing when his contract was not renewed. In other words, Roth had no property interest in continued employment. This case illustrates that at many institutions, and under the law of some states, nontenured university employees serve "at the pleasure of" or "at the will of" the controlling board or president and do not have constitutional due process rights. An institution may separately create these rights contractually with a written document or through its policies or procedures (Hustoles & Duerr, 1994).

The depth of due process protection
When a protected liberty or property interest is found to exist, the depth of the process that is due in any given case varies, depending on the nature of the case and the seriousness of the property or liberty interest at hand. Where, for example, a case involving the continuation of employment turns on the testimony of a single witness and indications are that the witness may be biased, the opportunity to directly confront and cross-examine that witness may be required. But where the proof in the case is less tenuous or where lesser interests are at stake, the courts allow considerable restriction of the right to cross-examine witnesses. Some courts, for example, have required students or teachers accused of misconduct to submit proposed questions to a hearing officer, who then conducts the examination of witnesses as he or she sees fit (Rubin & Greenhouse, 1983). The questioning of witnesses could even be conducted by the hearing officer outside the presence of the person being provided a hearing, who could later be provided with a summary of the adverse testimony. All the Supreme Court has said definitively is that procedural due process requires, at a minimum, that the deprivation of a protected property or liberty interest "be preceded by a notice and an opportunity for a hearing appropriate to the nature of the case" (*Ross v. Pennsylvania State University,* 1978, p. 153).

Public university administrators must therefore consider the nature and seriousness of each case they confront and adapt hearing procedures to the particular circumstances

---

involved. This process involves balancing the interests of the person receiving due process against the interests of the university in efficient, expeditious hearings. Because both these interests may be substantial, the administrator must usually factor in the value of any particular safeguard (such as the right to an attorney or the right to cross-examination) in preventing an erroneous decision. This "balancing test," formulated in the administrative law cases of *Goldberg* and *Mathews,* assists in determining the applicability and depth of particular due process safeguards. According to the Court in *Mathews:*

> *Identification of the specific dictates of due process generally requires consideration of three distinct factors: First, the private interest that will be affected by the official action; second, the risk of an erroneous deprivation of such interest through the procedures used, and the probable value, if any, of additional or substitute procedural safeguards; and finally, the Government's interest, including the function involved and the fiscal and administrative burdens that the additional or substitute procedural requirement would entail.*
> (1976, p. 335)

This formula can be simplified. To determine whether a particular safeguard is due, one first balances the governmental interest against the private interest involved. In other words, what the government stands to lose is compared with what the citizen has at stake. If one of these interests completely eclipses the other, the analysis is simple. But when, as is usually the case, both interests are significant, the formula becomes more complicated. One must then consider the chances that an incorrect decision might result from whatever procedure the government proposes or has in place, and how much that risk could be reduced by instead using the additional procedural protection urged by the citizen. If the process suggested by the citizen could easily be provided by the government (i.e., be provided in an economical and administratively simple manner) and that change would clearly result in more accurate decision making, then the citizen's position should prevail under the balancing test. On the other hand, if a safeguard sought by the citizen would place an undue economic or administrative burden on the government and the use of that safeguard would not appreciably increase the chances that a correct decision would result, then the government's existing procedure should remain in place.

Public and private institutions

For purposes of litigation addressing the denial of rights, the distinction between public and private universities is largely a distinction between proceeding on grounds of due process and an action based on contract theory. The development of case law has expanded the responsibility of public colleges to meet the rigorous standards of both procedural and substantive due process (Latourette & King, 1988). At the same time, the rights of students at private schools have grown substantially as courts have increasingly recognized an implied contract requiring that colleges act reasonably toward those they have agreed to educate. Although some courts have extended constitutional protection to students at private schools and the courts increasingly analyze cases in higher education in contractual terms, a fundamental legal difference remains between public and private universities.

As noted, a public university is an arm of state government and therefore falls under the legal authority of the Due Process Clause of the Fourteenth Amendment. When cases against public universities are brought, the required "state action" is present and a plaintiff can legitimately allege that a constitutional right has been violated. Specifically, the Fourteenth Amendment protects individual rights and liberties from arbitrary infringement by state government, and when an alleged deprivation of a protected interest results from action "under color of state law," a legal cause of action exists. This cause of action is quite different from a cause of action based on contract theory. A student's admittance to a private university implies a contract that if he or she pays the required fees and complies with the academic requirements prescribed by the school, he or she will be awarded a certain educational degree. Although a private school has the legal authority to discipline or even expel the student if he or she breaks the rules or is academically deficient, the school has the basic contractual obligation to act in a reasonable manner; a private college cannot legally deny a student a degree on arbitrary or unreasonable grounds. This same contract theory applies to legal action by professors or employees of private institutions. Increasingly, the courts analyze both private and public school cases in light of the principles of contract law (see *Ross v. Pennsylvania State University*, 1978). The provisions of the implied contract between universities and students are found primarily in the official documents promulgated by the school. To determine the process due in a particular case, the courts carefully examine a school's student and faculty handbooks, statements of policy, and rules and regulations. A university may also be bound by the procedural precedent it established in previous cases, even if its procedures are unwritten.

Although students at public universities have legal grounds for due process claims beyond those of students at private schools, administrators at private colleges cannot ignore the courts' constitutional interpretations. When a private school publishes its intent to provide due process in academic or disciplinary matters, it will be held to the same substantive and procedural standards required of public schools. Even when a private school does not promise due process, the reasonableness requirements of contract theory increasingly mirror the due process requirements of constitutional law. Americans often become so obsessed with questions of constitutionality that they give insufficient attention to considerations of wise policy (Wright, 1969). In the context of higher education, a wise university may well make a prudential judgment that it ought to give its students greater freedom, or more procedural protections, than the Constitution demands of it (Wright, 1969).

Student due process rights
Although the development of due process in the context of higher education has involved all members of the university community, the courts have placed special emphasis on the nature of the relationship between students and colleges (Wright, 1969). This relationship involves distinctive historical precedents, psychological constructs, and legal theories. The traditional view was that the university stood in loco parentis to the student. Under this legal doctrine, a school acted in the role of a parent and was assumed to possess the power to discipline wayward students for their own good. Because the courts respected this relationship, it was rare for a judge to intervene in educational decision making, and universities were allowed to have vague rules governing students' conduct. With the advent of the civil rights move-

ment and increasing judicial concern for individual constitutional rights, however, significant changes occurred.

In *Dixon v. Alabama State Board of Education* (1961), a court examined the expulsion from a public university of a group of Black college students who protested racial segregation policies in Montgomery, Alabama, by participating in marches and demonstrations. School regulations authorized expulsion for "conduct prejudicial to the school and for conduct unbecoming a student or future teacher in schools of Alabama, for insubordination and insurrection, or for inciting other pupils to like conduct." The federal court of appeals for the Fifth Circuit focused on the vagaries inherent in this language and the failure of the school to provide the students with any type of hearing in ruling that public universities must generally observe the requirements of due process before imposing disciplinary sanctions on students. *Dixon* brought about a new era of respect for the constitutional rights of students, fundamentally changing the relationship between students and institutions of higher education.

With the advent of the civil rights movement and increasing judicial concern for individual constitutional rights, however, significant changes occurred.

The response of many colleges and universities to *Dixon* and the subsequent cases adopting its mandate for due process has been to adopt increasingly detailed and precise codes of student discipline, with the result that the disciplinary systems on many campuses have become "mired in legalistic disputes over rules of evidence" (Lamont, 1979, p. 85). This problem has been blamed in part on college and university attorneys who fail to explain to campus officials that court cases describing due process requirements do not necessarily demand the full-blown adversarial hearings that now prevail at some institutions of higher education (Pavela, 1985). Although it is better to err on the side of providing too many procedural safeguards rather than too few, due process inquiries can be efficient, even elegant proceedings, using procedures that sharply focus the hearing on precise issues.

In attempts to avoid unconstitutionally vague regulations, many universities attempt to spell out exactly what conduct is unacceptable and exactly what procedural rights and safeguards will be provided to students who are charged with misbehavior. The conventional wisdom has been that to treat all students fairly and to avoid charges of unequal treatment, a single procedural scheme should be adopted for all incidents of misconduct and that this scheme should be strictly followed in each case.

The move to clarify what kinds of *conduct* are prohibited by university rules and regulations is a positive development, the legacy of the carefully crafted decision in *Dixon*. Public and private institutions of higher education should reasonably notify students in advance as to the behavior for which disciplinary sanctions will be imposed. The effort to specify a set procedure that must be followed whenever universities address such behavior, however, is legally misguided and often counterproductive. A one-size-fits-all procedure for disciplinary cases involving students is a misinterpretation of the requirements of due process, imposing a rigidity never required nor recommended by the U. S. Supreme Court. By its nature, due process is flexible in application, and hearing procedures should be adapted to the individual circumstances of each case. To require, for example, that a right to cross-examination be provided in *all* disciplinary cases involving students is as erroneous as holding that such a right can *never* be allowed.

It is clear that due process requires fair notice of charges and a meaningful opportunity to be heard in response to those charges. But that notice and hearing may be provided in a variety of ways, depending on the potential penalty involved and the facts and circumstances in each case. Therein lies the failing of many student disciplinary codes, because by requiring specific procedural safeguards (such as the right to cross-examine adverse witnesses, the right to "subpoena" witnesses or documents, or the right to assistance from an attorney or a faculty adviser) in every instance, these codes forsake the opportunity to adapt the hearing to the special circumstances of each case.

Consider again, for example, the right to cross-examine witnesses. In many cases, this right is essential. When guilt turns on the testimony of a single individual and there is reason to believe that this individual harbors bias or ill will toward the subject of the disciplinary proceeding, excellent reasons exist to allow rigorous, face-to-face confrontation. It may be the only way to test the veracity of the witness in some cases. But in many other situations, direct cross-examination serves little purpose. In *Dixon,* for example, the court specifically stated that at the hearing required for the expelled students, a right to cross-examine witnesses was not necessary. Such a right would actually have added little to the quest for justice in that case, because there was apparently little dispute that the students had participated in civil rights demonstrations. Far more important to the students in that case would have been an unrestricted opportunity to present evidence in their own defense. Student codes rarely address such rights, and, arguably by their silence, these codes deny a variety of procedural safeguards that could be crucial in various individual cases.

The essence of due process is a meaningful opportunity to be heard. But this meaning is different in different cases. The argument in favor of rigid student disciplinary codes of procedure implies that institutions of higher education will be forced to provide at least minimal due process if they must routinely provide a set of procedural safeguards. Simply increasing the number of procedural safeguards available at a student disciplinary hearing, however, does not in itself necessarily increase the student's opportunity to be meaningfully heard.

In fact, most schools now face a greater risk of being sued for violating their own complex regulations than for violating the simple standards of basic fairness that are all the judiciary actually requires (Pavela, 1985). "A better understanding of the due process requirements in student disciplinary cases should begin with the concept that the amount of due process should be in proportion to the penalty [that] might be imposed" (pp. 41-42). This principle holds true not only in disciplinary cases involving students, but also in the various other instances on campus when decisions to punish must be based on disputed facts.

The best approach to protecting an institution of higher education from legal liability involves educating the entire university community (administrators, faculty, and students) about the true nature of due process. When the concept is seen not simply as a legal requirement, but also as a practical method by which disputes can be fairly resolved, an appreciation for the value of due process can develop.

Academic and Disciplinary Sanctions
Academic evaluations
The Supreme Court has clearly distinguished the depth of due process protection necessary in academic decision making from the more stringent protection due when institutions of higher education impose penalties for disciplinary reasons. In *Board of Curators of the University of Missouri v. Horowitz* (1978), the Court ruled that because a university

apprised a student of her academic deficiencies and gave her several fair opportunities to correct her problems, no formal hearing was required before her dismissal. Academic evaluations were seen as more subjective and evaluative than the factual issues in a disciplinary case and not well suited for adjudicative procedures.

In a landmark case, *Regents of the University of Michigan v. Ewing* (1985), the Court reaffirmed the traditional respect that judges have traditionally afforded the professional judgment of educators regarding the academic competence of their students. In this case, a student challenged his professors' determination that he was not academically qualified to continue his medical studies. The Supreme Court confirmed that even when faculty provided the minimal due process protection involved in an internal review of the student's progress, their decision would not be disturbed unless the student could show a clear violation of substantive due process:

> *When judges are asked to review the substance of a genuinely academic decision, such as this one, they should show great respect for the faculty's professional judgement. Plainly they may not override it unless it is such a substantial departure from accepted norms as to demonstrate that the person or committee responsible did not actually exercise professional judgement.* (1985, p. 513)

Later court decisions have reiterated the general policy that genuine substantive evaluation of a student's academic capabilities is a matter beyond the scope of judicial review (see *Susan "M" v. New York Law School,* 1990). Although it is thus very difficult for a student to mount a successful legal challenge to decisions about academic competence, it would be incorrect to say that students have no due process rights in this regard. The court in *Susan "M"* indicated that if a student can demonstrate bad faith, arbitrariness, capriciousness, irrationality, or a constitutional or statutory violation with respect to a particular grade or academic evaluation, the courts can and should intervene. To make such a showing, a student at a public institution of higher education would necessarily have to be provided with fair notice of the relevant academic rules, notice of his or her alleged academic deficiencies, and an opportunity for some kind of hearing. Although the nature of such a proceeding could be informal, for example providing the student with an opportunity to explain his or her position to a departmental chair, the requirement for at least minimal due process remains. As discussed later, students at private institutions would have only the due process protection that may arise under contract law. A recent summary of the law on academic decision making concludes that the courts will not interfere if students have received notice of academic rules and if an institution's policies, processes, and practices do not depart substantially from accepted academic norms (Ford & Strope, 1996).

Disciplinary decisions

The situation is different when institutions of higher education impose penalties on students for violations of student conduct rules, such as rules regarding drinking, drugs, mischief, or sexual conduct. It can generally be said that the due process requirements for disciplinary sanctions are higher than those for academic decisions. In these situations, the flexibility of the due process standard is emphasized, and the process due depends on the severity of the proposed penalty. For example, if a public institution alleges that a student engaged in misconduct that warrants dismissal or expulsion, *Dixon* and its progeny require a fairly sophisticated process, including reasonable notice and a hearing that provides the student with a fair opportunity to confront the evidence against him or her. Although such a hearing involves far less procedural protection than a full-dress judicial inquiry, the student may be entitled to such procedural safeguards as cross-examination, the right to call his or her own witnesses, or even appointed counsel. As the severity of the proposed disciplinary sanctions decreases, however (for example, when suspension rather than dismissal is contemplated), the depth of the procedural protection required by due process becomes less. As stated in *Goss v. Lopez,* even high school students facing long-term suspension from public high schools are entitled to at least minimal notice and an opportunity to be heard in response to the allegations against them. And unless the situation involves danger to other students, the opportunity for some kind of hearing is usually due before the imposition of the suspension. To determine the appropriate depth of the due process protection required in a given situation requires first, compliance with the particular institution's established rules and policies, and second, an informed decision from among many potential procedural safeguards about what procedure is necessary under the particular circumstances. As is the case with academic decision making, both public and private institutions of higher education must follow their published regulations and act in a reasonable manner, not arbitrarily or capriciously.

Discipline related to academic performance
Often it is not possible to separate student misconduct from academic decision making, as in cases of cheating and plagiarism. For purposes related to due process, because these cases usually revolve around issues of disputed fact, they are generally treated by the courts as disciplinary actions rather than academic evaluations. Allegations of cheating against students can be more stigmatizing and have a greater impact on their future than allegations of nonacademic misconduct (Cole, 1994). Therefore, in cases when students' misconduct is "inextricably mixed with academic matters," public institutions should observe the more stringent due process procedures that would normally follow in purely disciplinary cases (p. 14).

Constitutional Competence in Higher Education

To protect themselves and their institutions from civil liability, those who make discretionary decisions in the higher education setting need a basic familiarity with the various bases for legal action and the rights that arise from federal statutes and constitutional law. More important, educational "administrators" (and this term is used in a broad sense to describe professors, department chairs, deans, and others who make decisions about disputes in higher education) need to understand that these rights are protected by the constitutional guarantee of due process of law. This section refers to a basic understanding of civil rights and an appreciation for the application of due process principles as "constitutional competence" (Rosenbloom & Carroll, 1990). This competence on the part of educational administrators involves both the ability to recognize *when* it is necessary to provide due process and an understanding of *how* due process can actually be provided in a given case. Although this report is focused primarily on the latter of these competencies, educational administrators should know enough about civil and constitutional rights to recognize situations that give rise to the need for due process protection. It then

remains for these educators to acknowledge these rights when they arise and respond to them in good faith. In the official positions and actions they take, constitutionally competent educational administrators seek to provide substantive due process by responding to alleged legal or constitutional violations in an objective, unbiased manner, and procedural due process by providing an appropriate mechanism to accomplish a fair hearing in each case.

Plaintiffs who contend that institutions of higher education have violated due process usually frame litigation in terms of a deprivation of civil rights. These rights may exist under the protections set out in the Constitution or under specific federal laws. When citizens allege that these rights have been violated, the claims may include assertions that substantive or procedural due process was denied. Most common are allegations of civil rights violations under Section 1983 of Title 42 of the U. S. Code. For example, a student who was expelled from a publicly funded university solely because he criticized a school's athletic policies might sue for reinstatement as a student and for money damages, based on the violation by the state university of his federal civil rights. This student's "cause of action" would exist because the student alleges that his First Amendment right to freedom of speech was violated. Compare this instance with a case filed by a student in a wheelchair who was unable to take a class because it was held in a classroom inaccessible to her. This disabled student might have a cause of action against a public or a private institution because endorsable rights are created by the federal Americans with Disabilities Act. As a final example, consider a student who was expelled from a public university because she was found to have hacked into her professor's computer to obtain answers for her next exam. This student might challenge the action taken by the university by way of a civil rights claim, alleging in court that she did not commit this violation, that the university did not hear her defense in a meaningful way, and that she was therefore wrongfully deprived of educational rights. Such a lawsuit invokes both the substantive due process claim that she did not commit the violation and the procedural due process allegation that the hearing into the matter conducted by the school was constitutionally deficient.

It is obvious to most administrators in public and private institutions of higher education that legal problems would be likely to result from official action that punished a student or faculty member solely because that person exercised his or her freedom of speech. Similarly, even though the Americans with Disabilities Act has been on the books for a relatively short time, educational administrators should be aware that their institutions may not legally engage in knowing or intentional discrimination on the basis of disability. Of course, the disputes that arise on college campuses are not always so clear that administrators can immediately perceive the applicability of constitutional and statutory laws.

The Court applies a standard of "reasonableness" when evaluating the constitutional rights of students and faculty members, weighing the intrusion on constitutional rights against the legitimacy of the pedagogical concerns involved. Reasonableness governs, for example, in cases when issues of academic freedom are raised. Whether or not academic freedom, in and of itself, is protected directly by the Constitution has been extensively debated (Katz, 1983; O'Neil, 1983b; Van Alstyne, 1972). For several decades, the Supreme Court has recognized and guarded the academic freedom of university professors, but the exact nature of the link between academic freedom and First Amendment freedom of speech remains unclear (Yudof, 1987). Courts attempt to balance the interests of the state against the value of free expression (Poch, 1993).

The law is also uncertain with regard to the extent that officials in higher education are immune to, or legally protected against, lawsuits. During the 1970s, the federal courts substantially revised the legal doctrine that presumed public administrators had absolute immunity from civil suits for violations of individual rights. In *Wood v. Strickland* (1975), the Supreme Court held that school board members who had expelled several public high school students without hearing evidence were legally entitled to only "qualified" good faith immunity:

> *The official must himself be-acting sincerely and with a belief he is doing right, but an act violating a student's constitutional rights can no more be justified by ignorance or disregard of settled, indisputable law on the part of one entrusted with supervision of students' daily lives than by the presence of actual malice. . . . A school board member . . . must be held to a standard of conduct based not only on permissible intentions, but also*

Whether or not academic freedom, in and of itself, is protected directly by the Constitution has been extensively debated . . .

on knowledge of the basic, unquestioned constitutional rights of his charges. (pp. 321-322)

The Supreme Court found that in the specific context of school discipline, a school board member is not immune from liability if he knew or reasonably should have known that the action he took within his sphere of official responsibility would violate the constitutional rights of a student, or if he took the action with the malicious intention to cause a deprivation of constitutional rights or other injury to the student. Qualified immunity exists depending on the scope of discretion and the responsibilities of the parties asserting the immunity. In other words, administrators and others involved in decision making in higher education have immunity only when they act within their discretionary powers, in good faith, and in a reasonable, rather than reckless, manner (Schwartz, 1991). Under current judicial doctrines, public administrators are required to abide by the settled constitutional principles and laws that are relevant in the context of their official duties. "Even routine, day to day administrative activities are now frequently regulated directly by constitutional concerns" (Rosenbloom & Carroll, 1990, p. 2). These comments are directed to all public administrators but are especially relevant in the field of higher education. Public administrators are expected to possess a fundamental understanding of the American constitutional framework as well as a grasp of the substantive rights that federal laws create.

Summary

The phrase "due process" is extraordinary in Anglo-American jurisprudence, involving both a philosophical tradition and a compelling historical significance. Due process has been the basis in American law for the protection of a wide range of criminal and civil rights. The Supreme Court has carefully maintained the viability of due process; it can be applied in new situations because it is vague, but this vagueness has frequently made the meaning of due process difficult to understand. The broad scope of the concept has frustrated efforts to precisely define its meaning or to quantify its parts, especially in the area of higher education.

The Fifth and Fourteenth Amendments to the United States Constitution protect citizens from the government's arbitrary deprivation of "life, liberty, or property without due process of law." The laws by which American government operates are required by the constitutional principle of "substantive due process" to be equitable and just. Similarly, the legal rules and procedures used to implement the law must be rational and fair, or a violation of "procedural due process" may occur. The requirement that the government provide due process exists whether the setting is a courtroom murder trial, an administrative agency proceeding, or a hearing being conducted by a publicly funded university.

Due process rights arise when protected property or liberty rights are violated. The courts perceive due process violations of protected property interests when schools suspend or expel students in ways that violate internal grievance procedures (Bienstock, 1996). In other cases, protected liberty interests have been implicated when universities dismissed college professors in ways that threatened their reputations or their ability to obtain other teaching positions (Baez & Centra, 1995).

The importance of due process in higher education continues to evolve. Literally thousands of legal cases have addressed this historic constitutional concept over the past several decades. Although these decisions sometimes conflict with each other, fundamental principles have emerged that can guide decision makers as they exercise discretion. By avoiding arbitrary or capricious decisions and by employing the procedural safeguards appropriate in each individual case, administrators in institutions of higher education meet the requirements of the law as well as the ethical responsibilities of their profession.

A SYSTEMIC APPROACH TO DUE PROCESS
IN HIGHER EDUCATION

This section describes a "systemic" approach to providing due process in the context of higher education. The provision of appropriate procedural safeguards begins with a planning model—a process. For each individual case, the approach requires a series of decisions that, when considered in an informed manner and executed in good faith, will protect the concerns of substantive due process and simplify the selection of appropriate procedural safeguards. The approach requires analyzing the nature of the problem, reviewing existing institutional policies and procedures, and balancing the claims involved. To determine which procedural safeguards need to be provided in hearing a case, the interests of the university student, professor, or employee must be weighed against the interests of the educational institution. Moreover, in accordance with the Supreme Court's standard of reasonableness in weighing the intrusion on constitutional rights against the legitimacy of pedagogical claims such as academic freedom, one must also consider the value of any specific procedural safeguard in reducing the risk of reaching an erroneous decision. (Appendix A presents a scenario describing the application of due process in higher education; Appendix B discusses *Nash v. Auburn University* [1987], a lawsuit brought by two students alleging that their procedural and substantive due process rights had been violated in a case involving cheating on a final exam.)

The approach to due process described here is called "systemic," because it is intended to apply throughout a university's academic and administrative hierarchy. It is systemic also in that it proceeds according to an organized plan. The approach is based primarily on the Supreme Court's decisions in the field of education that set out a scheme for due process protection. The philosophy underlying this approach is idealistic; it requires good faith efforts on the part of administrators (and here that term includes anyone who directs or facilitates the resolution of disputes in higher education). The courts expect that administrators will strive to structure meaningful inquiries that will lead to fair decision making and that they will recuse themselves from the process if they are unable to act without bias.

This approach conceptualizes discretionary decision making as a process involving active participation by those who will be affected by the outcomes of proceedings, and it assumes that administrators will recognize the importance of the dignity of each individual involved in the resolution of disputes in higher education. Thus, this approach provides a model by which the legal requirements of due process can be obtained in each case while addressing larger concerns about the role and mission of the university in modern society. By following this approach, administrators enhance opportunities for fair resolution of disputes, lay foundations for positive responses to the decisions they render, and prepare for legal challenges that may develop.

Decision Making in Higher Education

To choose rationally between conflicting versions of facts, regardless of the nature of the dispute, a judge or an administrator must hear the substance of both sides and weigh one against the other. The method by which a case is heard can influence the ultimate decision. Different nations and cultures have developed different systems of justice to structure the way in which judges hear cases, and institutions of higher education have formulated diverse rules about how cases related to education will be heard.

No set of written policies and procedures can completely anticipate all the procedural and evidentiary issues that will arise as cases are heard. In evaluating both sides, a judge (or an administrator in the context of higher education) must make a series of decisions, before and during the hearing of each case. For the sake of fairness and efficiency, these decisions should allow the presentation of as much relevant evidence as possible while excluding the presentation of irrelevant, extraneous material.

A primary responsibility of American judges is to decide which evidence should be considered and which should not be heard; judges can spend years training for this task. Under the American adversarial system, a judge's rulings can be subjected to intense scrutiny and reversed on appeal if determined to be incorrect. Professionals in the field of higher education, however, are rarely trained to make evidentiary rulings, and their determinations cannot be held to the same standard as judges. The courts recognize this distinction and do not demand that hearings in higher education be perfect in the evidentiary sense, or even that they reach the level of fairness required in criminal or civil trials. Rather, in light of the interests involved and the availability of later recourse to the legal system, the Supreme Court has emphasized the flexibility of the due process standard in the context of higher education.

A typical due process hearing in higher education

> . . . *involves a hearing panel, an administrator assist-*
> *ing the panel with various administrative duties, a*
> *complainant (the person who brought the complaint*
> *that triggered the formal process), and a respondent*
> *(the employee whose decisions or conduct the com-*
> *plainant is challenging). . . . While there is some ex-*
> *change of information between the complainant and*
> *the respondent, each of them is primarily interacting*
> *with the panel. Typically, the complainant is a person*
> *with less institutional power than the respondent, some-*
> *times significantly less.* (Bienstock, 1996, p. 1)

Bienstock identifies "typical" complainant-respondent pairs, such as a faculty member denied tenure and the provost, a student accused of theft and the dean of students, and an administrative assistant who was terminated and the director or vice president who approved the termination (1996, p. 1). Although these illustrations are helpful in picturing hearings in higher education, it is difficult to generalize when it comes to the parties involved or the appropriate procedural format.

Different circumstances call for different procedural safeguards. For example, when a student is alleged to have cheated on a classroom test, institutional rules may require the dean of students, a student honor code officer, the classroom professor, or some other official to present the case. This presentation may require important strategic decisions about which witnesses to call and how aggressively to conduct cross-examinations. Ultimately, the administrator's decisions regarding procedural format and safeguards will be the most important factors in determining the character and validity of the hearing. The following approach to due process encourages administrators to anticipate potential problems and structure hearings that will provide the parties involved in educational disputes with meaningful opportunities to be heard.

In the resolution of disputed facts, administrators must safeguard the dignity of each participant in the hearing. Although the American adversarial trial system invites aggressive and confrontational tactics, there is no reason for judges to allow rude behavior. Similarly, it is the responsibility of administrators in higher education to control the conduct of those who participate in hearings. Emotions can run high.

By demonstrating an overriding concern for fairness and compliance with the principles of procedural due process, an administrator can structure a hearing that will be perceived as fair by those involved in disputes. Such an approach fits within the emerging tradition of "alternative dispute resolution," which emphasizes creative problem solving and meaningful communication. This approach requires recognition of the flexible nature of the due process standard as well as integrity and creativity in formulating a procedure that will result in justice and understanding.

An Overview of the Systemic Approach

As illustrated in Figure 1, a comprehensive approach to due process in higher education involves compliance with two fundamental principles: *substantive due process,* or the overall fairness inherent in the decision, and *procedural due process,* involving the selection of specific procedural safeguards that are reasonable and appropriate for each individual case. To comply with these principles, this approach requires the consideration of several broad questions within the two areas.

FIGURE 1

A Systemic Approach to Fair Decision Making

SUBSTANTIVE DUE PROCESS

SDP-I: Are applicable university regulations reasonably clear in explaining the kinds of conduct that are required or prohibited and the sanctions that will be imposed if the regulations are violated?

SDP-II: Is the operation of the applicable university regulations in this case likely to result in a fair decision, one that is neither arbitrary nor capricious?

SDP-III: Does insurmountable institutional bias exist that precludes internal resolution of this case?

PROCEDURAL DUE PROCESS

PDP-I: What level of procedural complexity should generally govern the conduct of the hearing in this case?

INFORMAL MODEL	ADVERSARIAL MODEL	LITIGATION MODEL

➡————INCREASINGLY COMPLEX OR DISPUTED FACTS————➡

PDP-II: Who should decide the issues in this case, and how should the decision maker be chosen?

ADMINISTRATOR	SINGLE HEARING OFFICER	PANEL OR TRIBUNAL

➡————INCREASINGLY COMPLEX OR DISPUTED FACTS————➡

PDP-III: What potential procedural safeguards should be provided by due process in this case?

	Prehearing *PDP-III-A*	During hearing *PDP-III-B*	Posthearing *PDP-III-C*
Safeguards related to procedural format	•Separate investigation •"Plea bargain" •Routine postponement of hearing	•Open or closed hearing •Tape-recorded proceedings versus official notes versus recap in hearing decision versus oral summation	•Separate determination of penalty •Appeal within institution
Safeguards related to notice	•Obtain documents •Take depositions •Obtain witness list	•Be present during all testimony •Have the opportunity to object to testimony and evidence	•Written hearing decision indicating reasons for decision and facts determined to be true
Safeguards related to the opportunity to be heard	•Compulsory process for witnesses	•Unlimited opportunity to present evidence •Indirect participation or full participation of attorney or adviser •Full or partial cross-examination	•Opportunity to present appellate arguments in person, in writing, through an attorney
Safeguards related to substantive fairness	•Individual hearing officer versus tribunal •Opportunity to influence selection of decision maker •Independent decision maker •Opportunity to obtain exculpatory information •Adversarial procedure	•Witnesses under oath •Opportunity to object to evidence •Protection from self-incrimination	•Standard of proof (beyond reasonable doubt, substantial evidence, preponderance of evidence) •Standard on appeal (arbitrary, clearly erroneous, unwarranted)

Using this approach, an administrator confronting a decision that will result in institutional action that could potentially have adverse consequences for some member of the institutional community proceeds through the six numbered questions posed in Figure 1. Three questions are relevant for substantive due process (SDP on the figure). The administrator first reviews the institution's existing policies and rules to determine which are applicable to the particular case, ensuring that the applicable regulations are not obscure or overly vague (SDP-I on the figure). Assuming that the applicable rules are reasonably clear, the administrator considers the operation of those rules in the case at hand (SDP-II). Finally, to meet the demands of substantive due process, the administrator looks at the existence of personal or institutional bias that might play a part in the decision in the case (SDP-III).

With regard to procedural due process (PDP), an administrator first determines the general level of procedural formality that will apply throughout the notice, hearing, and appeal stages of the case (PDP-I), and then the identity and authority of the decision maker (PDP-II). Finally, the administrator decides the procedural safeguards that will be followed during the three phases of each case: before the hearing (PDP-III-A), during the hearing (PDP-III-B), and after the hearing with regard to a possible appeal (PDP-III-C). Figure 2 defines the specialized terms that are used in this discussion.

FIGURE 2

Definitions

> **Administrator.** Any person authorized by an institution to conduct or resolve internal disputes at any level of university administration—a classroom professor, a member of an academic committee, the chair of a department, a dean, a provost, an ombudsman, or another officer of an institution charged with responsibility to provide due process in disputes arising within the institutional community. Depending on the nature of the case being considered, the administrator may perform some, all, or none of the functions of the hearing officer, the decision maker, and/or the prosecutor or complainant.
>
> **Allegations.** Statements that describe a respondent's wrongdoing or the respondent's failure to take required actions, which are contained in the notice and about which proof is offered by the prosecutor or administrator at the hearing.
>
> **Appeal.** A fair and meaningful review of an adverse hearing decision at a higher level of the institutional hierarchy, and the mechanism by which that review is accomplished.
>
> **Decision maker.** The hearing officer or hearing panel that decides the hearing issues in a due process hearing. The deci-

sion maker may be the administrator, the hearing officer, or the tribunal in any particular case. The decision maker issues the hearing decision.

Hearing. An opportunity for a respondent to be heard in opposition to the charges or allegations.

Hearing decision. The official ruling on the hearing issues and allegations in a particular case. The hearing decision is usually in writing, but it may be announced orally. It should address each allegation contained in the notice and should describe opportunities for appeal and deadlines.

Hearing issues. Statements contained in the notice that define the scope of the hearing.

Hearing officer. An individual who presides over a due process hearing. After considering the evidence presented at the hearing, the hearing officer prepares the hearing decision. Depending on the decisions of the administrator or the policies and regulations of the institution, the hearing officer may be authorized to decide evidentiary, format, and procedural issues during the hearing, and may be authorized to determine the penalty to be imposed upon a finding that the allegations in the case are true. The hearing officer may also act as the prosecutor.

Hearing panel. A group of people who preside over and decide the hearing issues in a due process hearing. The panel may comprise any two or more students, faculty members, administrators, officials, or other members of an institutional community. Used interchangeably with "tribunal."

Institution. A public or private college or university in the United States. The words "university," "college," and "institution" are used interchangeably.

Institutional community. All persons taking courses at, hired by, or otherwise affiliated with the institution.

Notice. An oral or written communication from the administrator to the respondent providing enough information about the charges or allegations so that the respondent can prepare a defense.

Prosecutor. The person who presents proof of the allegations against the respondent at the hearing. Depending on the nature of the case and its procedural complexity, the administrator may perform the function of the prosecutor or designate another individual for this purpose.

Respondent. A member of an institutional community whose conduct becomes the subject of a potential sanction by the institution. The respondent may be a student, faculty member, or any other type of employee at an institution.

Reviewer on appeal. The official who conducts the review of an adverse decision.

Tribunal. See *hearing panel.*

An Approach to Substantive Due Process

> **SDP-I:** Are applicable university regulations reasonably clear in explaining the kinds of conduct that are required or prohibited and the sanctions that will be imposed if the regulations are violated?

As indicated, a higher education administrator's first task, when confronted with a dispute, is to consult and consider the applicable institutional rules and regulations. In some cases, institutional policies may refer to and incorporate state or federal laws, or they may be modified by precedents set in previous cases. Administrators must be familiar with the sources of policy affecting their institutions, and they must consult with counsel or other administrators to determine these sources. Existing institutional policy may provide an administrator with substantial procedural guidance, as is often the case in tenure disputes at publicly funded universities, or the institutional regulations may simply direct that due process be provided, as is sometimes the case when cheating in the classroom is alleged. In any event, existing regulations are always the starting point in resolving disputes in higher education, and established policies should be followed strictly unless adherence would produce manifest injustice.

Once an administrator identifies the applicable institutional regulations, those regulations should be evaluated in light of the case at hand. The administrator must decide whether the rules give fair warning to those governed by them. For example, in *Dixon v. Alabama State Board of Education* (1961), a state university expelled students who participated in protest demonstrations against racial discrimination in Montgomery, Alabama. The school board contended the expulsion was justified because the students violated a regulation prohibiting students from engaging in conduct that would reflect badly on future teachers. A federal circuit court, in a ruling later affirmed by the Supreme Court, held that such a vague standard did not provide proper notice as to what conduct was actually prohibited. As this case illustrates, administrators and university counsel should regularly review existing regulations to ensure that they are clear and fair with respect to the conduct of those they govern.

After determining that applicable university regulations are sufficiently clear, an administrator should examine the specific operation of the rules in the case at hand. Substantive

> **SDP-II:** Is the operation of the applicable university regulations in this case likely to result in a fair decision, one that is neither arbitrary nor capricious?

due process requires that a university's action, seen in the totality of the circumstances, be fair. In some cases, applicable regulations, although reasonable on their face, will result in an obviously unfair outcome. Because due process is a flexible standard, administrators must use good judgment to determine how existing policies should be interpreted in each case to bring about a just result. Thus, written procedures may need to be modified and adapted to particular circumstances. When written procedures guarantee certain procedural steps, those procedures must be strictly followed, but when substantive fairness demands additional safeguards beyond those prescribed in written rules, administrators should not hesitate to expand procedural rights and protections in an appropriate hearing format.

> **SDP-III:** Does insurmountable institutional bias exist that precludes internal resolution of this case?

The final requirement of substantive due process under this approach is related to the requirement that administrators in higher education act in ways that are not arbitrary and capricious. This decision is related to a subsequent procedural determination—the identity of the decision maker in the case—but should initially be seen as an issue involving broad, substantive fairness. Occasionally a case arises in which a university's interests or reputation is so threatened that its decision will be suspect regardless of the procedural precautions actually provided. For example, a case might arise in which a university president or trustee is charged with wrongdoing. As question SDP-III implies, even decisions involving highly placed university officials could be made internally if extensive procedural precautions are employed. In other situations, however, a university might have to acknowledge that it is unable to fairly decide an issue and relinquish decision making to an outside, unrelated authority.

Because due process is a flexible standard, administrators must use good judgment to determine how existing policies should be interpreted in each case to bring about a just result.

An Approach to Procedural Due Process

In *Goss v. Lopez,* the U. S. Supreme Court ruled that students in a public high school were entitled to "minimal" due process

procedures—notice and some kind of hearing—before being
suspended. A decade later, the Court in *Board of Curators of
the University of Missouri v. Horowitz* limited the *Goss* precedent to only those suspensions and dismissals that were imposed for reasons of misconduct rather than for reasons of
academic incompetence. In *Horowitz,* the Court made it clear
that due process required that a continuum of procedural complexity be available in higher education settings; it held that far
less procedural protection was required for academic suspension or expulsion, as compared with disciplinary dismissal.

Golden (1982) researched the procedural protections that
were actually afforded in academic and disciplinary hearings
in higher education, examining doctorate-granting institutions,
comprehensive universities, liberal arts colleges, and professional schools. The ways that schools provided notice, the
degrees of procedural protection offered at hearings, the opportunities allowed for appeal, and the levels of formality of
the hearings provided varied widely. Defining "informal"
hearings generally as office meetings with administrators and
"formal" hearings as those where additional procedural protections beyond such office meetings (usually involving a
hearing panel or some other explicit right), Golden found that
doctorate-granting institutions provided the highest level of
procedural hearing safeguards in the disciplinary area. Professional schools appeared to provide slightly more procedural hearing protections in the academic area, while liberal
arts colleges provided significantly less academic procedural
hearing protections than the other three institutional types (p.
351). These procedural variations underscore the need for
reasoned, justifiable decisions about the level of due process
observed in each institution of higher learning. A university
should strive not only for objective fairness in its procedures,
but also for internal consistency of its system, respecting the
precedents it has established in previous cases.

A systemic approach to procedural due process begins with
consideration of the overall level of complexity that is appropriate in each individual case. Three models of procedural
complexity are briefly described in the following paragraphs.
They should be conceptualized as points along a continuum
of complexity, ranging from the minimal due process of an

informal, two-sided discussion to the extensive procedural protection exhibited in the trial of a felony under American criminal law. In such a criminal trial, given that long-term incarceration or the taking of a citizen's life by the government is possible, more process is normally due than would ever be the case in a matter arising in higher education. Nonetheless, important property or liberty interests may be at stake in the educational setting. By considering the relative seriousness of these interests, an administrator first conceptualizes the case before him or her in terms of the following models.

Litigation model

To Americans, the most familiar adjudicatory procedure to resolve a dispute is the adversarial trial. Under this approach, two opposing parties present their cases to a neutral judge according to formalized rules of evidence and procedure. The decision of the judge is binding, subject to appeal. In rare instances, it may be necessary for administrators to structure hearings similar to adversarial trials. Because this process is rigid and based on conflict, the litigation model demands relatively detailed notice and discovery techniques, a trial-like format, and the use of extensive procedural safeguards throughout the process.

Resort to the litigation model should be limited to those situations where the relationship between the institution and the respondent is irretrievably broken and where the institution seeks to sever the existing relationship. In a case, for example, in which criminal charges are pending against a professor for the manufacture of illegal drugs using university property, extreme measures are warranted. Or when a student has been charged with committing an assault in the classroom upon another student or a professor and permanent expulsion may be the final outcome, resort to the litigation model may be necessary. In such cases, the university, working with a state prosecutor, may need to arrange for counsel for the respondent. An independent hearing officer, someone from outside the institutional community, may also be needed. Similarly, when a university expects that a disgruntled employee will bring legal action regardless of the method by which a dispute is resolved, the litigation model, employing extensive procedural safeguards, is advisable.

The role of the administrator during the hearing under this model is to facilitate the proceeding, assisting and providing information to the parties and the hearing officer. An attorney for the institution acts as the prosecutor and assumes the burden of proof. When criminal charges are pending or could arise, the institution should provide the respondent with an independent attorney.

Adversarial model

This level of procedure involves an orderly but less formal hearing than the litigation model. Based on clear but not highly detailed notice, a hearing officer hears testimony from witnesses, receives pertinent documents, considers the parties' arguments, and, on this basis, renders a written decision.

This model is very flexible with respect to the actual procedural safeguards used. It is appropriate for disputes for which serious penalties are contemplated. In an adversarial proceeding of this nature, although both parties to the dispute must have the opportunity to present their positions to the hearing officer, the hearing officer has discretion to limit the length of the presentations. The hearing officer may choose to limit the number of witnesses, the length of witnesses' testimony, the availability of attorneys or advisers, and the extent and method of cross-examination. Disputes that range in importance from the very serious to the very minor may be resolved using this level of procedural formality.

Informal model

In some European countries, judges play a vigorous role in the resolution of disputes, leading a fact-finding inquiry. Under this inquisitorial procedure, examining magistrates make independent investigations before trial, then dominate the conduct of the proceeding and the questioning of witnesses. This approach to fact finding can be efficient and cost effective while providing the essential elements of due process. Under this informal approach, an administrator might act as hearing officer and prosecutor to confront a respondent with allegations of wrongdoing. In a multifaceted role, the administrator must be aware of the possibility for bias, but there is no reason that this level of procedural complexity should result in less than fair notice or in a less than meaningful opportunity to be heard. Despite the narrower focus that the adoption of this model involves, decisions about individual procedural safeguards must still be individually considered by an administrator. An informal hearing could retain many of the hallmarks of an adversarial trial, such as the opportunity to cross-examine witnesses in some manner and the assistance of an adviser. This model might be appropriate in disputes in higher education when the potential penalty is less than expulsion or termination, or in cases when an "advisory" or supplemental opinion from a committee about the proper resolution of a case is sought.

An administrator's choice as to the level of procedural complexity appropriate for the case at hand involves an initial appraisal of the nature and relative seriousness of the case. This early decision does not necessarily govern later choices about explicit procedural safeguards, but it does indicate the administrator's perception of the general character of the matter. This determination will help define ongoing strategy for the case.

> **PDP-II:** Who should decide the issues in this case, and how should the decision maker be chosen?

A hearing before an unbiased tribunal is traditionally recognized as a basic requirement of due process. The courts expect that in hearings in higher education, reasonable efforts will be made to prevent the probability of unfairness that arises when an individual who is biased decides a case (Rubin & Greenhouse, 1983). Although an impartial decision maker is essential for due process, the courts have allowed educational institutions considerable discretion as to the composition of tribunals and the identity of hearing officers. A tribunal may comprise any number and combination of students, faculty members, or administrators. A hearing officer is a single individual who may be from within the institutional community or, rarely, from outside that community.

The choice between a tribunal and a hearing officer depends first on whether a particular institution has rules that specifically govern in the circumstances of the case. Almost all institutions have academic codes and faculty handbooks that designate decision makers in various circumstances. Frequently, for example, the decision-making power in tenure procedures is clearly delegated. Less frequent but still common are specifications for tribunals or hearing officers in academic disputes. When specific rules exist, they should be strictly followed. If, however, as is frequently the case, an institution's policies are unclear or silent as to the identity of

the decision maker in a particular kind of case, the administrator should analyze the situation by balancing the potential
loss faced by the respondent against the need for an independent tribunal. The administrative burden and cost to the
institution of delegating decision-making power must also
be taken into account.

With regard to a respondent's interests, it can be specu-
lated that generally a tribunal offers greater objectivity and
impartiality than a single hearing officer. Moreover, allowing
a respondent a voice in, or even control over, the selection
of the decision maker is a way to reduce bias, or the appearance of bias. But such a procedural safeguard reflects a
case of a very serious nature. With regard to the institution's
interests, there is little question that the use of a tribunal
rather than a single hearing officer increases the logistical
burdens, financial and administrative costs, and the amount
of time required to resolve a dispute. And when the respondent has a role in the selection of the decision maker, time
becomes a concern because a new set of disputes could
arise during selection.

Balancing the options involves consideration of the increased impartiality of a tribunal in which the respondent
has a voice compared with the relative efficiency and procedural simplicity offered by a single hearing officer. The administrator must, in light of these interests, decide whether a
tribunal is significantly more likely to reach a fair result in
the particular circumstances of the case at hand. The courts
have generally trusted institutional judgment with respect to
the objectivity of the decision makers they select. Obviously,
it would violate due process if a decision maker had a financial interest in the outcome of a hearing or when personal
animosity or prejudgment on the decision maker's part
could be shown (Rubin & Greenhouse, 1983). The test the
courts apply is whether the decision maker was actually
biased, rather than whether there was the potential for bias
or the appearance of bias (Stoner & Cerminara, 1990).

> **PDP-III-A:** What procedural safeguards should be provided
> before the hearing?

The right to an open hearing

An "open" hearing is one conducted in a public forum and
announced in some manner so that members of the institu-

tional community, the public, and representatives of the media might attend. A "closed" hearing, in contrast, is one attended by only those considered necessary and authorized by the administrator or hearing officer. The results of a closed hearing would not be made public or would be announced only in general terms.

The Family Educational Rights and Privacy Act of 1974 (FERPA), also known as the Buckley Amendment, not only grants students access to their official institutional files, but also restricts the release of certain information about students by institutions. Under FERPA, only appropriate "school officials" with a "legitimate educational interest" may access students' records without the consent of the student (Hollander et al., 1995). Thus, the release of information in the course of a hearing open to the public or to the institutional community about disciplinary action taken against a student or about a student's alleged misconduct may violate the law. The extent to which universities may "publish" or release such information has become highly controversial, and it is possible that the reporting requirements of a relatively new federal law, the Campus Security Act, as well as some state "sunshine" laws requiring public decision making to be done in open meetings may conflict with the protection of privacy created under FERPA.

Additionally, conducting an open hearing may give rise to a separate violation of protected liberty interests, beyond the immediate issue of the hearing. As described earlier, the meaning of "liberty" for purposes of due process is broad. The Supreme Court has indicated that when a person's good name, reputation, honor, or integrity is at stake because of what the government is doing to him or her, a liberty interest protected by due process may arise (Pavela, 1985). By holding an open hearing and thereby making the hearing issues public, an institution may open itself to charges in the nature of libel or slander. These concerns exist whether the respondent is a student, faculty member, or another type of employee of the institution.

By allowing only those who are essential to be present when a hearing is conducted, an administrator protects both the institution and the respondent's confidentiality. On the other hand, a respondent may request that the hearing be open so that the allegations and the actions of the institution are available for scrutiny. An institution may also be in favor of open hearings to demonstrate that the procedures it uses are fair or to deter another person from committing the same act. In light of the legal issues raised by open hearings, however, it is recommended that due process hearings be closed, that is, conducted in a manner that protects the privacy of the respondent. If an open hearing is conducted, the respondent's written consent should be obtained.

The right to discovery

A litigant in a civil case may use several devices to learn details of his or her opponent's case. "Discovery" devices, such as oral depositions, written interrogatories, and requests for documents can ensure fairness, encourage settlements, and improve the efficiency of trials (Gellhorn & Boyer, 1981). In higher education cases, some courts have found that prior disclosure of relevant documents and reports was necessary for fair hearings to take place. For example, when a tenured teacher was placed on involuntary leave because of an alleged mental problem, a school board was required to furnish her with copies of the medical reports on which it relied (Rubin & Greenhouse, 1983).

Courts generally measure the extent to which records and other documents should have been provided to a respondent in terms of the actual prejudice the respondent suffered by not having the documents available at the hearing. When the courts review an administrator's decisions about the need for discovery, the administrator's judgment is usually given deference unless the respondent can show that he or she was actually damaged by not being allowed to discover a certain item before a hearing.

The proliferation of discovery, the formal procedural methods by which parties obtain information about each other's case, has been blamed for backlogs and skyrocketing litigation costs in American courts. Reasonable arguments exist both for and against allowing limited discovery in disputes in higher education. Discovery procedures may enhance fairness in that a respondent has more precise notice of the charges to which he or she must respond. But providing a respondent with a right to review or obtain information about the case before the hearing can result in delay and increased administrative burden.

It is not difficult to imagine a case in which a limited right to discovery would be appropriate. In a dispute about tenure or a disciplinary action against a faculty member where numerous prior complaints or evaluations make up the bulk of the proof to be offered in support of the institution's position, a prehearing right to examine these and other internal documents would be in order. Or in a case in which a student faced an institutional disciplinary hearing involving actions that could also be criminally prosecuted as a felony, an opportunity to engage in discovery before the hearing might be legally necessary.

An institution's legitimate interest in limiting a respondent's discovery rights includes the protection of information not relevant to the respondent's case, the potential delay inherent in discovery procedures, and the time and expense involved. In the special case of depositions, sworn oral statements taken before a hearing, an institution would be legitimately concerned with the lack of control over the scope of a deposition and the potential for invasion of the privacy of the individual being deposed.

The respondent's interest in obtaining discovery before the hearing coincides with the fundamental due process requirement of fair notice as to the charges one faces before defending oneself. Clearly, the concept of fair notice requires that a respondent be advised, before the hearing, of the nature of the adverse testimony to be presented. Moreover, as reliance on documentary evidence in a case increases, the argument in favor of documentary discovery becomes stronger. When proof of the allegations involves voluminous or complicated documentary evidence, a respondent would have a good argument that those documents should be provided before the hearing. But hard and fast rules about the extent of discovery allowed are not possible. The nature of each particular case must determine the balance between the conflicting interests of the respondent and the institution. It can be said, however, that by voluntarily providing all relevant information and documentary evidence before the hearing, institutions minimize the need for discovery.

The right to exculpatory evidence

As investigations proceed into matters that are potential subjects of due process hearings, administrators may discover information favorable to the respondent or indications that the respondent may not be at fault. This information may be in the form of conflicting accounts from witnesses, documents supporting the respondent's version of the facts or casting doubt upon witnesses against him or her, or other kinds of evidence. Because the institution is in a superior position to obtain such information, a respondent may not become aware of certain facts or defenses unless the institution takes affirmative steps to reveal what it has learned.

In the criminal justice process, such information is called "exculpatory" evidence—evidence that tends to show the defendant is not guilty of a crime. The existence of exculpatory material raises difficult evidentiary and ethical questions. Different people have different views about the duty of a prosecutor, for example, to reveal that a star witness has a previous criminal conviction or harbors bias that is unknown to the defendant. In the context of criminal law, certain detailed rules concern the right to discover exculpatory evidence. Such rules do not exist for disputes in higher education, however. Thus, administrators should always take affirmative steps to reveal information that is even arguably exculpatory to the respondent.

The right to compulsory process

To defend against the allegations brought against a respondent, the respondent may require the testimony of witnesses who are reluctant to appear at a hearing. An institution has a strong interest in protecting members of its community from needlessly appearing at hearings or being required to testify based on unreasonable demands. On the other hand, the respondent may be able to show that testimony from a reluctant member of the institutional community is relevant and important to his or her defense. In such cases, the institution may legitimately use its resources and influence to require such testimony. Administrators may, however, require that any request for such testimony be presented by the respondent well before the date of the hearing so that its relevance and availability can be considered. Steps may be taken to protect reluctant witnesses. It would be a violation of fundamental due process rights to allow anonymous testimony, although as indicated later, an administrator may limit the extent to which witnesses are subjected to cross-examination in appropriate circumstances.

The right to an independent investigation

A preliminary investigation by a committee to determine the appropriateness of proceeding with certain allegations is an extreme step, which will be necessary only under rare circumstances. The preliminary inquiry contemplated here would go beyond the internal administrative investigation that will normally take place in any case. An independent investigation could be compared with the function of a grand jury in the criminal justice system. The grand jury operates as a check on the power of the prosecution to require a defendant to undergo the expense and ordeal of a criminal trial. Similarly, a charge of serious misconduct in higher education, even when confidentiality is maintained, involves a considerable ordeal, and an objective evaluation may be justified in rare cases. Although little incentive usually exists for administrators to lightly bring charges requiring due process hearings against students or employees, in certain circumstances an administrator would be wise to convene an independent committee to investigate and review the need for a hearing, to dispel even the appearance of impropriety.

A due process hearing is itself an investigation into charges or allegations, and the conclusions drawn from a hearing are normally subject to reexamination on appeal. Nonetheless, extraordinary cases, which might be called "political," can arise, and the individual circumstances in each case need to be considered to determine whether a screening committee for certain allegations might be necessary. Consider, for example, a situation in which the editor of the student newspaper at a public institution is alleged to have violated university regulations by publishing an editorial that was not only critical of school athletic policies but also potentially libelous with regard to a particular coach. In such a situation, the appointment of an ad hoc university committee to consider the nature, legitimacy, and appropriateness of each potential allegation against the student could have an important function. Such a committee could dispel, to some degree, the appearance of bias that might naturally arise.

As with all potential procedural safeguards, the need for a prehearing, independent investigation should be determined through an analysis balancing the pros and cons. The administrative burden involved in convening an investigative committee varies depending on the depth of the investigation and the nature of the case. A respondent might frame the need for a separate investigating committee as an issue involving substantive fairness. Such an argument could suggest that the charges were brought against the respondent as harassment rather than

. . . extraordinary cases, which might be called "political," can arise, and the individual circumstances in each case need to be considered to determine whether a screening committee for certain allegations might be necessary.

on merit. Although an administrator could address such charges in the course of the hearing, in certain rare cases the need for a separate investigation becomes obvious. If a student or professor, for example, has been critical of the institution in an unrelated matter or had a history of disagreements with the university administration, a separate committee to investigate new charges before a hearing might be appropriate.

The right to postpone a hearing

A request from a respondent to postpone a hearing may be framed in terms of the need for adequate time to prepare a defense or in terms of the adequacy of the notice provided. Due process in educational cases generally requires that respondents be provided a reasonable amount of time in which to prepare to defend themselves against charges. Courts have, for example, reversed the results of university hearings into serious charges when notice was delivered only a day in advance (Rubin & Greenhouse, 1983).

A request to postpone a hearing may be accompanied by a request for additional information about the allegations, compounding the issue of the adequacy of the institution's notice to the respondent. In a case where the only charges against a school superintendent were that he was incompetent and had willfully neglected his duty, a court held that such notice was insufficient for purposes of due process (Rubin & Greenhouse, 1983). Other courts have indicated that even when respondents know of the allegations from other sources, they are nonetheless entitled to clear notice from institutions. Because fair notice is a fundamental requisite of due process, administrators should accommodate a request from a respondent for additional information about the allegations whenever the request is reasonable. But postponement of a hearing for other reasons need not be automatically granted. The institution's interest in expeditiously completing hearings must be weighed against the respondent's reasons for postponing a hearing in each case.

> **PDP-III-B:** What procedural safeguards should be provided during the hearing?

The right to a recorded hearing

The procedural safeguard involved in creating an accurate account of the hearing is important in relation to any appeal that may occur. If a case is to be meaningfully reviewed, by way of an administrative appeal or by a court, a record of the case must be preserved. Although a review could be conducted based on a comprehensive hearing decision (that is, one that recounts who testified at the hearing and summarizes the evidence that was presented), the creation of an independent record of the hearing allows for a more accurate evaluation of the testimony and arguments presented at the hearing.

A record of the hearing may be created by mechanical means (audiotape or videotape recordings) or by taking notes during or after the hearing. Institutional rules commonly require that due process hearings be tape-recorded. The tape may be transcribed for reading, or the reviewing authority may simply listen to the tape. Although a standing rule that all hearings be taped has some obvious advantages in terms of objective accuracy, it also has some disadvantages. In cases when the potential sanction is minor and affects lower levels of administration (such as in the classroom or before an advisory committee), a written summary of the evidence presented at the hearing is more manageable and convenient.

The competing interests with respect to the creation of a mechanical record, as opposed to notes, involve the administrative burden versus the opportunity to develop arguments on appeal. The respondent often desires a comprehensive record that will fully describe the evidence and arguments presented during the hearing. A respondent generally desires the most precise account possible, preferring a mechanical recording over notes or a summary, which allows an argument that the procedures provided were inadequate to be more readily verified.

Although many of the same benefits that accrue to a respondent from a recorded hearing also apply to the institution, an institution may choose to provide only a summary of the testimony and argument for several reasons. It may prefer the relative ease of management that summaries provide compared with a recording. Even a brief hearing may generate a substantial record, and transcription involves certain costs. A strong argument can be made that efforts to limit paperwork are necessary and reasonable. Thus, it is recommended that records of hearings involving a classroom and hearings before advisory committees be kept as uncluttered as possible. Tribunal members and hearing officers at every level should also limit the quantity of personal notes taken during hearings. The production of such notes may be demanded at subsequent hearings, either within the institution or in court. If they have not been preserved, the appearance of impropriety may be raised; if they are produced and examined, unclear notes may raise unanswerable questions.

The format of hearings

Depending on the magnitude of rules at their institution, administrators in higher education have considerable discretion as to the structure of the hearings they conduct. Although due process requires some kind of hearing, the rules for how a hearing should proceed are general. The format of the hearing should be logical and reasonable rather than arbitrary and capricious. Because the format used for American criminal and civil trials is familiar, organized, and logical, institutional rules or customs often model hearings in higher education similarly. In an adversarial trial, an impartial judge presides over opposing attorneys, who present their clients' cases to a fact-finding entity (a jury or a judge). The charging party, called the plaintiff or the prosecutor, initially presents witnesses in support of certain allegations. The responding party may cross-examine the plaintiff's witnesses and, at the close of the plaintiff's case, may choose to present witnesses of his or her own, who are also subject to cross-examination. Both sides then have the opportunity to present arguments, providing their own interpretation of the evidence presented. In the American system, a jury then determines which facts have been proved and applies the law as directed by the judge.

In addition to the defendant in each case, three distinct actors in the American adversarial process can be identified: the judge, the prosecutor (or plaintiff in a civil case), and the fact finder (a jury or the judge.) The function of the judge is to preside over the trial and to decide questions of evidentiary procedure. The function of the prosecutor or plaintiff is to present evidence in support of the charges or allegations in the case. The prosecutor or plaintiff is said to have the burden of proof, or the responsibility to present a convincing case before the need for any evidence in response by the defendant. The function of the jury or judge is to determine which facts are accepted as true. Under a systemic approach to due process, these same three functions must be performed in each hearing. Depending on the nature of the case, an administrator may choose to delegate all these roles to others or act in all three capacities him or herself.

Although the basic structure of a trial is simple, the rules of procedure under the American adversarial system have become complex. Highly trained attorneys conduct trials, even at the lowest levels of the system, because evidentiary rules must be carefully followed if they are to perform their intended functions. When properly applied, the rules of evidence permit the consideration of relevant evidence and exclude irrelevant or unfair testimony. But if a judge or one of the lawyers involved in a case is inept in the application of the rules of evidence, the process can quickly deteriorate, leaving little hope for discovering the truth of the matter at issue. For example, under the Federal Rules of Evidence, some, but not unlimited, testimony about a person's character is allowed in evidence. In some cases, such testimony might provide valuable insight into the respondent's honesty and integrity and reflect on his or her propensity to commit the kind of act with which he or she is charged. But a parade of witnesses repetitiously proclaiming that the respondent is of excellent character is of little ultimate value for purposes of determining disputed facts. Therefore, the rules of evidence restrict the kind of character evidence that may be offered and allow the trial court judge considerable discretion in limiting repetitious or useless testimony. The judicial power also allows the exercise of judgment with respect to the number of witnesses presented and the extent of their testimony.

Administrators and decision makers charged with providing due process in higher education disputes are required to make similar choices. Due process requires a fair hearing of disputed facts, but a workable method for presenting those facts to the decision maker and at the same time excluding extraneous information from that presentation can be elusive. In other words, how should "relevance" be defined in practice? What limits are fair with respect to the number of witnesses a respondent may offer in a hearing in higher education, and what restrictions can be imposed upon the scope of their testimony? What happens if the respondent challenges a ruling made during a hearing? Such procedural questions should be considered before a hearing begins.

An institution has a clear interest in limiting the scope of a hearing. These proceedings can require enormous expenditures of time and resources. They may distract faculty from teaching and delay administrative staff in their pursuit of the university's mission. It is entirely legitimate for administrators to conduct hearings efficiently and succinctly, as long as they are fair. By providing precise allegations and sharply defined hearing issues, an administrator can begin to limit the scope of a hearing.

Administrators should also recognize that no trial or hearing is ever perfect. Important information will be excluded in some cases, and extraneous information will be allowed in others. The courts have never required that trials be flawless to comply with due process, only that they be fair. This same principle applies to hearings in higher education. For purposes of due process, all that the courts require is that the respondent be fairly informed of the charges or allegations he or she faces and that he or she be provided sufficient time and a meaningful opportunity to respond to them.

Reasonable alternatives exist to the traditional method of presenting evidence through the sworn testimony of witnesses. Written statements may be obtained from adverse witnesses. These statements could be provided to the respondent for a written or oral response. Or testimony may be taken outside the respondent's presence, then summarized and provided to the respondent. When emotions are high but facts are not in significant dispute, a decision maker might choose to hear independent statements from both the prosecutor and the respondent, then decide on certain areas in which limited cross-examination may be conducted. When an administrator believes that the opportunity to present evidence is being abused, he or she may place time limits on the testimony of witnesses or restrictions on the subject matter of testimony at the hearing.

The American adversarial system contemplates a process under which an impartial judge mediates the efforts of advocates for opposing sides in a dispute. The judge is essentially passive, listening to the arguments and evidence presented by the parties. When the parties to a hearing are not trained in rules of evidence, the potential for disorder and confusion during the proceeding increases. An administrator must foresee the possibility for unruly hearings and set ground rules at the outset. When necessary, provisions to prevent the interruption of witnesses and to limit repetitious evidence should be announced and enforced during the hearing. If a party to a hearing refuses to comply, the administrator may need to conclude the hearing and resume later in a more restrictive fashion. In certain cases, it is conceivable that a respondent could be required to present his or her evidence or respond to adverse witnesses only in writing. The benefits of such a requirement, orderliness and clarity, might outweigh the respondent's need for immediacy and the benefits that flow from the cross-examination of witnesses. A respondent could be required to submit proposed evidence or questions for witnesses to the hearing officer, who would then make an independent judgment about the admissibility of evidence or the need for each proposed question.

The adversarial system may not be the best model for fact finding in most disputes in higher education. A hearing may be more a conversation than a trial, although as the seriousness of the potential penalty in a case increases, the format of the hearing should increasingly be modeled on traditional adversarial procedure. Moreover, administrators should outline the hearing format they have decided upon when they provide notice in the case to the respondent.

The right to representation

In the general context of higher education, there are few clear rules about the legal right to an attorney or an adviser to represent a respondent during a hearing. When student misconduct that is the subject of a hearing is also the basis for a criminal prosecution, due process may *require* legal counsel for the student (Cole, 1994; Rubin & Greenhouse, 1983). Moreover, when the institution chooses to be represented by its attorney in a hearing, it is necessary that the respondent also be provided an attorney (Cole, 1994). Except in extremely serious cases where an attorney is clearly required, an administrator's decision about a respondent's need for an attorney or adviser and the proper extent of their involvement in the hearing can be difficult. To make the right decision about representation, an administrator should consider the nature and posture of the case, beginning with any instructions provided by institutional rules and policies. Frequently, model codes for university hearings and institutional rules expressly permit a respondent to be accompanied by an attorney or adviser. Under some codes, the representative is not allowed to speak on the respondent's behalf, only to advise the respondent during the hearing (Bienstock, 1996). Under other codes, legal representation is not required or specifically ruled out, so a discretionary decision must be made.

The right to an attorney or an adviser is a procedural safeguard intended to satisfy the requirement that a respondent have a meaningful opportunity to be heard. In many ways, this right is the ultimate procedural safeguard and the one with the greatest potential to delay, confuse, and extend hearings in higher education. After the U. S. Supreme Court granted juveniles facing delinquency charges the right to an attorney, legal commentators noticed an increase in the adversarial nature of juvenile court proceedings. The Supreme Court's decision in *In re Gault* (1967) unquestionably increased the procedural safeguards provided during juvenile court proceedings, but it has been criticized for reducing the power and inclination of judges to act in the best interests of juveniles.

The same kind of problems may arise when attorneys are involved in hearings in higher education. As attorneys use the procedures associated with due process, the adversarial nature of the proceeding and the time it takes to conduct the hearing increase. Whether the attorney participates directly or as an adviser during the hearing, lengthy cross-examinations, technical legal arguments, and new procedural accommodations and objections can be expected.

At least one author (Picozzi, 1987) takes the position that the increased administrative burden and the heightened adversarial nature of hearings involving attorneys are justified by the benefits that arise when legal counsel is provided for respondents in educational disputes. He proposes that in every case where the potential penalty involves any permanent mark on a student's record, the assistance of counsel should be allowed. Moreover, he asserts, universities play a "procedural game" with students, providing just enough process to fulfill the vague dictates of the law but not enough for the student to have a fair opportunity to defend himself or herself. And with respect to the right to counsel:

> *That procedural game is not only unconstitutional, it exposes the myth of universities acting objectively [toward] their students. There's nothing magically collegial about a university; once a student is charged, a full-*

*fledged adversarial relationship exists, and university
officials are like everyone else. They play to win.*
(Picozzi, 1987, p. 2150)

In balancing the competing interests with respect to the
assistance of counsel, an administrator should consider the
purpose of this procedural safeguard. Will the respondent
be able to meaningfully respond to the allegations in the
case at hand without an attorney? If the case is complex or
depends in large part on the testimony of a witness whose
veracity is questionable, the balance tips in favor of allowing
counsel. But in the majority of cases in higher education,
college students and faculty are competent to present their
own cases.

One final point should be emphasized with respect to the
provision of attorneys in educational disputes. As indicated
earlier, when a respondent's misconduct has become the
subject of criminal prosecution, the respondent has a right to
appointed counsel. In *U. S. v. Wade* (1967), the Supreme
Court held that any stage of criminal prosecution, formal or
informal, in court or out, when counsel's absence might dero-
gate from the accused's right to a fair trial is a critical stage
where counsel must be provided. Such situations should be
carefully coordinated between the institution and the state or
federal prosecutor involved as to the timing of the hearing
and the appointment of counsel. In this situation, it might be
necessary for the university to pay for an attorney for the
respondent. In a hearing where a respondent might make a
statement that could later be used in court against him or her,
the principles of the *Miranda v. Arizona* (1966) decision suggest that the respondent also has the right to remain silent.

The right to cross-examination
The right to cross-examination in a criminal case is a fundamental constitutional right; the Sixth Amendment requires that
a defendant have the opportunity to confront the witnesses
against him or her. Over the centuries, Anglo-American jurisprudence has promoted the art of cross-examination as a
reliable method for seeking truth. Cross-examination has three
purposes: (a) to challenge the credibility of the statements
made on direct examination; (b) to bring out additional facts
relating to those elicited on direct examination that were favorable to the opposing party; and (c) to give the trier of fact

an opportunity to observe the witness under stress (Klein, 1989, p. 59).

As the purposes of cross-examination indicate, undergoing formalized questioning under oath can become a psychological ordeal. An attorney skilled in cross-examination techniques can confuse and confound a witness and cast doubt on untruthful as well as truthful testimony. The potential exists for cross-examination, especially when it is conducted by an emotional individual who is untrained in the rules of evidence, to deteriorate into outright harassment and badgering. Most attorneys recognize that this kind of interrogation does not help their case and refrain from using cross-examination as an opportunity to simply argue with a witness.

Justice requires that institutions of higher education provide respondents with those procedural safeguards that will actually result in fair notice and a meaningful opportunity to be heard. Colleges and universities also have a legitimate interest in eliminating hearing procedures that interfere in the quest for truth. Cross-examination, perhaps more than any other procedural safeguard, has the potential for assuring veracity but also the potential for abuse. When a witness harbors bias or lies or does not tell the whole truth, no better tool exists than precise cross-examination to expose these testimonial defects. But cross-examination can also be used to intimidate and confuse witnesses and to distort forthright testimony.

A respondent almost always perceives the right to cross-examination as desirable, and can frame arguments in favor of extensive cross-examination in terms of proper notice. To respond to the allegations, a respondent may claim that he or she needs the opportunity to fully explore the testimony of each witness. In some, but certainly not all, cases, this argument has merit. Very few courts have required that respondents in higher education cases be provided with the right to unrestricted cross-examination of witnesses; indeed, many cases suggest that this right is not required to provide due process. As indicated earlier, when a case rises or falls based on questionable testimony, the right to cross-examination may be necessary for due process, at least with respect to crucial witnesses. In other cases, when cross-examination leads to disruption rather than illumination, alternatives such as allowing the respondent to submit proposed questions for the witness through the hearing officer or simply allowing the hearing officer to conduct the cross-examination himself or herself should be considered.

The right to sworn testimony

Requiring witnesses to swear or affirm that they will speak the truth when they testify is a recognized and common safeguard in a range of criminal, civil, and administrative proceedings. Although the liberty or property interests at stake in higher education hearings may not equal those involved in trials, they are nonetheless important. In most cases, it is in the interest of both the institution and the respondent to require that witnesses swear or affirm that the testimony they give will be truthful.

The right to refuse to participate or remain silent

The Fifth Amendment right against self-incrimination or "to remain silent" is a cherished constitutional safeguard that has been protected by the Supreme Court in various contexts. Suspects in criminal cases usually cannot be required to answer questions at any stage of the criminal justice process (from the earliest investigatory stage all the way through trial) if those answers might be incriminating. Public employees cannot be threatened with the loss of their jobs by conditioning continued employment on cooperation with criminal investigations.

In situations in higher education when activities that are the subject of a hearing might also lead to criminal prosecution, administrators must respect the constitutional right against self-incrimination. It would obviously be important for an administrator under these circumstances to work closely with the prosecutor who has jurisdiction over the potential charge so that the hearing does not interfere with a criminal case. If the hearing issues overlap with the elements of a serious criminal offense, an institution might delay its hearing in the matter until the criminal charge is resolved. If an administrator believes, however, that the respondent poses a danger to the institutional community, the administrator should immediately conduct a hearing to remove the respondent from the institution during the pendency of the criminal case (Pavela, 1985).

If a defendant/respondent is found not guilty on criminal charges mirroring those that are the subject of a hearing, the allegations could be considered resolved. An institution is also entitled to conduct its own hearing subsequent to a criminal trial without violating the constitutional prohibition against double jeopardy. Similarly, if a respondent is found guilty of a criminal charge, an institution may proceed with its own hearing into the violation of institutional rules, and penalties in addition to the government's criminal sanctions may be imposed.

Most cases of institutional discipline do not involve corresponding criminal charges, and the question arises whether the principle involved in the right against self-incrimination should generally apply in higher education cases—meaning that the tribunal or the hearing officer would be instructed that no adverse inference should be drawn from the respondent's refusal to offer testimony in his or her own defense. When a respondent chooses not to testify, relying on the weakness of the evidence in support of the allegations, the respondent might seek an instruction that no adverse inference should be drawn from his or her silence. The logic is that a respondent should not be punished by way of an inference of guilt simply because he or she exercised his constitutional right to remain silent in the face of the allegations. It is true that criminal defendants are presumed innocent and that a respondent should not be required to affirmatively prove his or her innocence, but it is also true that the degree of due process necessary in higher education hearings is significantly less than that required in criminal trials. Therefore, an argument based on constitutional self-incrimination has less merit in hearings into educational disputes than in the context of a criminal trial. If the purpose of a hearing is to explore all the relevant information involved in the dispute, the drawing of any logical conclusion seems warranted. Although a respondent should not be coerced into testifying against his or her will, it should generally be understood that whatever inferences seem appropriate to the decision maker under the circumstances may in fact be drawn from the respondent's silence. An important exception to this general rule arises in cases when the respondent may face a criminal prosecution based on the acts that form the basis for the allegations in a particular case. When possible criminal charges are involved, proceedings by a public institution should be seen as a part of governmental action in response to a crime, and institutional proceedings should be closely coordinated with the action of the local prosecutor.

Standards of proof

The law recognizes several different levels of proof with regard to whether a crime has been committed. To issue an arrest warrant or search warrant, a judge need only be presented with "probable cause" to believe the suspect committed a crime. If a judge believes, based on the facts presented, that the suspect *probably* committed the crime, an arrest or search is authorized. But to convict a defendant, a judge or jury must find proof "beyond a reasonable doubt" that he or she is guilty of a criminal act. This standard requires less than absolute certainty, but more than probable cause.

Between "probable cause" and "beyond a reasonable doubt," the law recognizes other quanta or degrees of proof. A standard of "preponderance of evidence" is used to decide who prevails in a civil action. Because money rather than a liberty interest or a defendant's life is at stake, due process allows a verdict in favor of whichever side produces the most proof—which is not to say that if a plaintiff presents five witnesses and the defendant has only three, the plaintiff necessarily wins the case. The judge or jury must evaluate the quality of the proof offered by both sides, then return a decision in favor of the side that presented more believable evidence than the other. "Clear and convincing" evidence is another standard of proof that lies somewhere between "preponderance of evidence" and proof "beyond a reasonable doubt." "Clear and convincing" requires more than the simple preponderance of evidence but still allows for some doubt on the part of the decision maker. The courts have also established a quantum of proof known as "substantial evidence" as the standard for a prosecution to prevail in an administrative hearing. In this context, "substantial evidence" means relevant evidence that a reasonable person might accept as adequate to support a conclusion, although other reasonable minds might not agree (Klein, 1989).

The courts have not determined that any particular standard of evidence is required to find against a respondent in the context of higher education hearings. Some student disciplinary codes specify a particular standard of proof for use in serious disciplinary proceedings, often adopting the "preponderance of evidence" or "clear and convincing" standards. A few schools have extremely strict disciplinary codes that demand the penalty of expulsion for any violation and, in light of this harsh mandatory penalty, require that the violation be proved beyond a reasonable doubt. The "clear and convincing" standard should be employed in all cases when serious disciplinary measures may be imposed (Picozzi, 1987).

Considering the risk of an erroneous hearing decision that may result from adopting a standard of evidence that is too low, good arguments exist for requiring at least the "clear and convincing" standard in the context of higher education. An administrator should consider the fact that such hearings rarely turn on "hard" physical evidence, such as fingerprints. Most often, cases in higher education require subjective judgments about circumstantial, testimonial evidence. Thus, the sufficiency of the evidence on which allegations are determined to be true involves an issue of substantial fairness. Because the outcome of a hearing can have a long-term influence on a respondent's life, there is good reason to adopt a rigorous standard for proof in higher education cases.

Finally, it should be noted that questions exist as to the meaning or validity of the use of various quanta of proof. Standards such as "clear and convincing" are necessarily vague and imprecise. What appears to be proof beyond a reasonable doubt to one person may amount to only a preponderance of evidence to another. It is important for an administrator to decide what standard will be used at the hearing and to at least discuss the meaning of that standard with the decision maker before the hearing. The issue of appropriate standards of evidence must be revisited when the administrator considers the level of evidence that should be required to overturn a hearing decision as the result of an appeal.

Setting penalties
When the allegations examined during a hearing are found to be true, a respondent may assert a due process interest in who actually determines the penalty to be imposed. The argument that due process requires this penalty be determined by the decision maker (hearing officer or tribunal) rather than by an administrator or other institutional officer finds little support in court decisions (Rubin & Greenhouse, 1983). When the penalty is said to be excessively harsh in

An administrator should consider the fact that such hearings rarely turn on "hard" physical evidence, such as fingerprints.

relation to the respondent's conduct or when bias on the part of the person determining the penalty is alleged, an appeal based on this substantive violation of fairness might successfully be raised. In cases involving the suggestion or appearance of institutional bias, administrators should consider leaving the determination of the extent of the penalty to be imposed to someone outside the institution or to an institutional committee selected for this purpose. Otherwise, institutions of higher education have considerable discretion in selecting who will determine the extent of a respondent's penalty. Before the hearing, an administrator should consider who will determine any penalty that may be imposed and include this information with the maximum potential penalty contemplated in the case in the notice to the respondent.

Specificity in the hearing decision

Hearing decisions may be challenged on appeal for reasons related to procedural or substantive due process. A respondent may suggest that he or she was denied an essential safeguard or a necessary step in the process and that therefore his or her right to procedural due process was violated. On substantive grounds, a respondent may allege that the hearing decision is simply not justified by the totality of the evidence presented at the hearing. Thus, to prepare an appeal, a respondent must know which disputed facts were determined to be true and the reasoning on which the hearing decision is based.

To understand the importance of a hearing decision that specifies the grounds upon which it is based, consider the difference between a jury verdict of "guilty" and a judge's written decision containing Finding of Facts and Conclusions of Law. Although a jury verdict may be appealed, the appellant is forced to make presumptions about the basis for the decision to assign grounds for appeal. The appellant must assume that the jury, for example, believed certain witnesses and discounted the testimony of others; the appellant must also speculate as to the jury's interpretation of the law and how it was applied in his or her particular case. Contrast such a "speculative" appeal with one in which a judge explicitly sets out the weight he or she gave to the testimony of each crucial witness at the trial as well as the specific legal reasoning he or she used to decide the case. Clearly, an appeal based on specific findings of fact and law can more precisely address the true issues in a case and present appellate judges with a better opportunity to render justice.

Precision in the construction and focus of an appeal benefits both an appellant and an institution in higher education cases. When both sides know the basis of a hearing decision, the appeal process becomes more efficient. For this reason, hearing decisions should specify those facts that the hearing officer determined to be true and the reasons the hearing officer ruled that way. Where possible, these reasons should refer to specifically cited institutional rules, regulations, and policies.

To construct a hearing decision along these lines, the hearing officer should first list the important facts found to be true in the case. When testimony conflicted about crucial facts, the hearing officer should set out the evidentiary reasons *why* he or she found those facts to be true, citing specific testimony and affirmatively accepting one version of the facts over another. This exercise may be the most difficult part of the hearing officer's task, but it is also one of the most important. The purpose of the hearing is for the hearing officer to listen to both sides in the dispute, then fairly and completely decide the hearing issues. When hearing officers accept this responsibility and render clear, decisive opinions, hearing decisions can be fairly evaluated on appeal.

Right to appeal and procedure on appeal

The right to appeal an adverse decision to a higher administrative level is not normally a fundamental element of due process, but under a systemic approach to due process, a right to appeal is essential. The decision-making structure in most colleges and universities is hierarchical. Decisions are usually the result of coordinated communication between professionals at various levels of the system. This structure implies that appeals will be available in some form. Additionally, the educational mission of American colleges and universities involves more than the transmission of information; it also involves an appreciation for democratic ideals and practical lessons in ethical behavior. In light of this mission, the question becomes *how* rather than *whether* the respondent will be informed of a right to appeal a hearing decision. As with all parts of the due process formula, how to communicate the right to appeal is flexible, but it is recommended that appeal rights be described in the hearing decision.

The purpose of the appeal is not to provide a second hearing in the case but to impose a safeguard against mistakes or the misuse of discretionary power at the hearing. Depending on the nature of the case, the review might examine the fairness of a hearing by simply evaluating the hearing decision, or it might include an exhaustive examination of all the testimony that led to the decision, entertaining written and oral arguments from the parties.

The respondent has an interest in an appeal process that includes a review of not only the substantive fairness of the hearing, but also the entire procedural mechanism that was used. The respondent might further argue that he or his attorney should be afforded the opportunity to present both written and oral arguments to the reviewer on appeal. And the respondent might further contend that the reviewer should be required to analyze the entire hearing with the aid of a videotape and/or a written transcript, suggesting a duty on the part of the reviewer to locate and address any unfairness or impropriety, whether the issue has been raised in the appeal or not.

Conversely, an institution has a legitimate interest in a limited and succinct appeal process. Rather than waiting for days, weeks, or months for an extensive review to take place, an institution would be expected to seek to expedite the appeal, requiring only that the reviewer read the hearing decision and respond to any obvious problems or errors. An institution could legitimately argue that *requiring* the reviewer to read transcripts of testimony or to watch a videotaped hearing in its entirety is no guarantee that a more sagacious analysis of that hearing will take place.

In most cases, the entire transcript or tape of the hearing should be available to the reviewer, but the extent to which he or she makes use of this resource should not be dictated. Depending on institutional rules and the seriousness of the penalty involved, the reviewer should retain discretion concerning the extensiveness of the review. Similarly, only rarely will oral arguments on appeal be necessary. In most cases, a written appeal in the form of a letter to the reviewer provides a sufficient opportunity to raise and argue the issues on appeal.

It is important that the respondent be informed as to how to undertake an appeal and about any time deadlines. These steps and deadlines may be generally set out in university regulations, but specific information and deadline dates for the appeal should be calculated by the administrator and communicated in the hearing decision.

Extent of sanctions

With respect to the requirements of constitutional due process, an administrator has great discretion in deciding who will determine the appropriate penalty to be imposed in the event that allegations against a respondent are determined to be true. University regulations sometimes specify a particular penalty for a particular offense or state who shall determine penalties within a specified range. To the extent an institution's regulations are not specific, an administrator should, early in the process, establish how the potential sanction in the case will be determined. The extent of the sanction may be left to the decision maker at the hearing, or the administrator may retain this power if he or she does not act as decision maker. The reviewer on appeal may be given the power to modify the penalty as part of the review.

Right to a transcript

To prepare an appeal, a respondent may argue it is necessary that the institution provide him or her with the complete record of the hearing. The rationale for such a position is similar to arguments in favor of requiring decision makers to state the facts and reasoning on which their hearing decisions are based. An argument of substantive fairness suggests that, without a transcript, the decision maker on appeal cannot determine whether the conclusions in the hearing decision are actually justified by the evidence.

If it has been decided to record the hearing rather than relying on notes or a synopsis of the testimony, it is usually necessary to have the record transcribed. Even if the respondent is unwilling or unable to pay for a transcript, a compelling case can usually be made that the institution should supply the document so that the respondent has an opportunity for a meaningful appeal.

Standard for review on appeal

The previous discussion of the standard of evidence to be used in determining the truth of the allegations in a case applies when the fairness and legitimacy of a hearing decision are considered on appeal. Just as the evidence supporting allegations considered at a hearing is required to meet a certain standard ("clear and convincing" or "preponderance of evidence"), the conclusions in the hearing decision must be subjected to an appropriate evidentiary standard.

In the context of administrative law, one of the most cursory standards for appellate scrutiny is whether the decision maker's conclusions were "unwarranted." Under this standard, the reviewer may substitute his or her interpretation of the facts and evidence for that of the decision maker simply because he or she disagrees with the conclusions set out in the hearing decision. This standard is problematic in that it undermines the force of the hearing decision and reduces the stability of the process, because decisions can be so easily overturned.

A higher standard would require that the reviewer on appeal overturn the hearing decision only when he or she demonstrates in writing that its conclusions are "clearly erroneous." An even greater standard would not allow the reviewer on appeal to overturn the hearing decision unless the reviewer found its conclusions so groundless that it could be characterized as "arbitrary and capricious." In other words, if the reviewer could find any rational support for the hearing decision, even if the reviewer did not agree with the outcome, the decision would be upheld.

It can be argued that the institution and the respondent are on equal footing with respect to the standard of review on appeal. Because either might disagree with the conclusions in the hearing decision, both might argue in favor of a lower appellate standard of review. But because the reviewer on appeal is usually an official of the institution, a respondent may argue that the standard on appeal ought to be, at the least, "clearly erroneous."

Summary

The foregoing catalog of procedural safeguards reviews a range of different formats and methods by which disputes in higher education may be heard. The flexible nature of the due process standard and the long-standing deference of the courts to academic decision making suggest that administrators will retain considerable discretion in the ways hearings are conducted. The wise exercise of this discretion involves not only concern for justice and fair play, but also administrators' ability to combine appropriate procedural safeguards in a sequence that will result in accurate decisions. An important component in this process is the pragmatic consideration of each potential safeguard and a cost/benefit analysis of the value each brings to the inquiry. A hearing format designed in light of the nature of the case and of appropriate procedural safeguards is the best defense against arbitrary and capricious decision making.

CONCLUSION

Toward the Therapeutic Application of Due Process

This report describes an approach to due process based on an analysis of the nature of disputes in higher education and the adaptation of a range of procedural safeguards to the needs of each particular case. Using this approach, administrators in higher education can undertake unbiased hearings that will result in accurate decision making. When pursued in good faith and with constitutional competence, these hearings will satisfy the requirements imposed by constitutional and contract law on institutions of higher education. But due process in higher education has another dimension, which is equally important.

Educators communicate a powerful message when they recognize the fundamental rights of persons who are accused of wrongdoing and afford them a participatory role in a process that includes a meaningful opportunity to be heard. By embracing the principles of due process at all levels of its hierarchy, a university demonstrates a commitment to fair play and participatory justice. But beyond the legal necessities are psychological and pedagogical reasons why such a philosophy is appropriate in higher education.

Wexler and Winick (1991) have developed a perspective that examines the potential for the law and legal processes to act in ways they call "therapeutic." The premise of "therapeutic jurisprudence" is that legal rules should encourage therapeutic outcomes when it is possible to do so without offending important values. This perspective grew out of reforms of mental health law, where the impact of the legal process on people was criticized because it often appeared to inflict great harm on those it was intended to help. Winick (1996) suggests that individuals' experience of the law may have damaging consequences or actually promote psychological well-being, allowing people to learn and grow. He holds that legal procedures, rules, and the roles of actors in the legal system (such as lawyers and judges) constitute social forces that, whether intended or not, often produce therapeutic or antitherapeutic consequences. "Therapeutic jurisprudence calls for the study of these consequences with the tools of the social sciences in order to identify them and to ascertain whether the law's antitherapeutic effects can be reduced, and its therapeutic effects enhanced, without subordinating due process and other justice values" (p. 646).

Using the perspective of therapeutic jurisprudence means that great potential exists for therapeutic consequences in higher education disputes. The psychological and pedagogical benefits that accrue from resolving disputes in accordance with the principles of due process further justify the institution-wide implementation of due process. In fact, an understanding of the principles of therapeutic jurisprudence may be fundamental to the implementation of due process in the context of higher education.

A growing body of literature has considered the psychological consequences of participating in various aspects of the judicial system and individuals' procedural preferences for the resolution of disputes (Lind & Tyler, 1988; Lind et al., 1990; Thibaut & Walker, 1975; Wexler & Winick, 1991). Among the findings in these studies is that the objective characteristics of a case, such as the amount won or lost, its duration, or the cost of the dispositional process, were generally unrelated to perceptions of the fairness of the procedure or to the degree of satisfaction participants expressed about the proceeding (Lind & Tyler, 1988). Instead, people are most strongly affected by their evaluations of the process itself. "People are affected by the way in which decisions are made, irrespective of what those decisions are" (Tyler, 1996, p. 6).

Studies suggest that experiencing legal policies or procedures perceived as unfair influences the extent to which people accept and abide by judicial decisions. A powerful example of this point is a description of the reaction of criminal defendants in drug prosecutions who lose any respect they may have had for the law when given the choice of informing on friends and family or serving sentences that are clearly excessive (Gould, 1996). Other research indicates that the experience of participation in a judicial hearing affects the extent to which a person respects the law and legal authorities. "When people believe that legal authorities are less legitimate, they are less likely to be law-abiding citizens in their everyday lives" (Tyler, 1996, p. 7). The legitimacy ascribed to judicial authorities is heavily influenced by a person's perception and evaluation of his or her experiences with judicial procedure.

It appears that one can live with a harsh penalty if it comes as the result of a process perceived as fair (or at least rational) much more easily than one can with the random, unprincipled imposition of discretionary power. This conclu-

A growing body of literature has considered the psychological consequences of participating in various aspects of the judicial system and individuals' procedural preferences for the resolution of disputes . . .

sion is supported by research into the perception of "control" and the damaging consequences of perceived helplessness or "learned helplessness" (Abramson, Seligman, & Teasdale, 1978; Maier & Seligman, 1976; Seligman & Garber, 1980). Thus, an important justification for the requirement of due process is to provide people who come into conflict with the government with at least some influence over their fate. In fact, the U. S. Supreme Court has recognized that due process is important not only because it leads to accurate decision making, but also because the denial of due process can result in psychological harm. In *Morrissey v. Brewer* (1972), the Court required that convicted criminals facing revocation of parole be provided with specific procedural safeguards not only for constitutional reasons, but also because the Court recognized that how these defendants were treated would influence their receptivity to efforts at rehabilitation. Similarly, in *Goldberg v. Kelly* (1970), the Court required procedural due process before the termination of welfare benefits not only because the recipients had protected property interests, but also because it recognized the psychological damage that the denial of due process would work on these citizens. The literature on therapeutic jurisprudence supports the Court's concern with the psychological impact resulting from peoples' experiences with the legal system.

In evaluating procedural justice, people seem to focus on attributes such as the neutrality of the decision maker, the lack of bias inherent in the conduct of the proceeding, and the decision maker's expertise. But at least three other aspects of procedure are more important in evaluations of fairness (Tyler, 1996): having an opportunity to participate in the process (usually by including a chance to present evidence), being treated with dignity as the process proceeds, and having a sense of trust in the decision maker.

Not surprisingly, it has been found that people perceive greater fairness in procedures in which they are allowed to present evidence over those where this opportunity is not provided (Lind & Tyler, 1988). It is interesting, however, that this observation holds true even when people are aware that their presentation will not affect the decision in the proceeding. Presenting evidence apparently has value or meaning in and of itself.

It is also clear that people respond psychologically to the respect, politeness, and dignity they are afforded during official proceedings. "People value the affirmation of their status by legal authorities as competent, [equal citizens] and human beings, and they regard procedures as unfair if they are not consistent with that affirmation" (Tyler, 1996, p. 10).

Finally, when people trust that those who are conducting official proceedings are concerned about their welfare and want to treat them fairly, they are much more likely to perceive the proceeding in which they are involved as fair. Trust is apparently an important component in the perception of legitimacy in official proceedings, because people have a need to believe in the benevolence of authorities. This belief allows for stability and faith in the prediction of future societal interactions. "If people infer a benevolent disposition in some authority, they can trust that, in the long run, an authority will behave in ways that serve their interests" (Tyler, 1996, p. 11). This trust is so powerful that people can experience unfair treatment, such as sexism or racism, without reporting that the procedures involved were unfair if they infer that the authorities involved were motivated to treat them fairly (Tyler & Lind, 1992).

The implications of research into the therapeutic consequences that may result from judicial proceedings are important for decision makers in higher education. If respondents in disputes in higher education perceive that they have no control over the penalties imposed upon them, or if they are not treated with dignity as they experience an institution's disciplinary process, they are more likely to lose respect for the institution and to seek to avoid whatever outcomes result from those institutional procedures. In practical terms, this likely outcome means an increase in litigation and a decrease in effectiveness in achieving the pedagogical objectives of the university. Conversely, an institution that voluntarily and affirmatively seeks to provide due process before imposing discipline begins to create a climate where education, in its highest intellectual and moral sense, can flourish.

Educators should concern themselves with the moral development of students (Pavela, 1985).

The values affirmed through the disciplinary process include a respect for individual freedom and the obligation to make a constructive contribution to the life of the community. The end result of these efforts may be

*the finest product of the educational enterprise: free,
mature, and responsible human beings.* (pp. 51-52)

This result can occur in the university environment because,
although we endeavor to protect students from arbitrary
decision making, we also challenge them to adhere to a fair
but strict standard of personal conduct (Pavela, 1985). Instead of fearing the conflict that results from challenge,
Pavela proposes that we appreciate the capacity of dissent
and dispute to stimulate growth.

Even as higher education becomes increasingly commer-
cialized, this conception of the university environment and
mission can prevail. At some universities, it may seem naive
to suggest that the administration might forgo its legal authority to coerce compliance with its policies in favor of a
system of decision making based on trust and participation.
But a vital belief remains in most colleges and universities
that higher education is a sacred trust. The systemic approach to decision making proposed in this report encourages those involved in participatory hearings to explore the
nature of justice. Resolving disputes in higher education in
accordance with the principles of due process is a time-
consuming and demanding enterprise, but ultimately this
approach is the most accurate, fair, and rewarding one.

Recommendations for Policy and Practice
Although each institution must determine its own standards
and needs when it comes to making decisions about disputed facts, the approach based on principles of due process described in this report is strongly recommended for all
colleges and universities. The following suggestions are
offered for the implementation of principles of due process
in decision making in higher education:

 1. *Existing due process policies should be examined and
    modified if necessary to achieve a balance between speci-
    ficity and flexibility in the procedural safeguards to be
    provided in each case.* It is impossible to prescribe what
    procedural safeguards will be appropriate before exam-
    ining the nature and potential penalty involved in each
    case. Although institutional policies and procedures for
    resolving disputes according to principles of due

process should be published and promulgated at all levels of university administration, these statements should be framed in general terms. Rather than specifically promising the right to an attorney or the right to cross-examination when disputes arise, university policies should describe a commitment to due process.

A prompt and thorough investigation in accordance with principles of due process is obviously required when a formal complaint or grievance is presented by a student or other member of the university community. But even when a problem is not presented formally, a university may still have the obligation to address instances of discrimination or harassment if it were on notice that the problem existed. Most recently, the U. S. Supreme Court discussed this requirement in the context of Title IX of the Education Amendments of 1972, which prohibits sex discrimination in federally supported education. In this context, the Court requires that school officials affirmatively confront not only "teacher-student" harassment, but also "student-on-student" harassment when it is so severe that it has the effect of denying the victim equal access to an educational program. Institutions should consider the number of complaints received as a "barometer of the campus climate" and undertake campus-wide strategies to prevent future incidents (Williams, 1999, p. A56).

2. *Administrators in higher education should make an institutional and an individual commitment to the provision of due process when disputed facts are examined.* "Good faith" is an indispensable element of due process in higher education. Rather than viewing the requirements of constitutional due process as an obstacle course or a lawyer's trap, administrators should strive to examine disputed facts accurately and fairly. In doing so, they will in most cases fully comply with the requirements of the law.

3. *All institutional decision makers should be trained to recognize situations when the principles of due process are appropriate and be familiar with the range of procedural options by which those principles may be applied.* Situations involving disputed facts arise and evolve at different levels within the university hierarchy. As classroom professors, committee members, or hearing offi-

cers, university employees should recognize their responsibilities to act in accordance with due process. This awareness comes only when a university undertakes an affirmative program to educate its employees about its policies and procedures, and to train its employees in the practical application of those polices. Because the requirements of due process are flexible and vary according to circumstances, professionals in the field of education should learn the ways in which the courts have authorized hearings for academic and disciplinary disputes. Such training requires a commitment of time and resources by the university and its employees.

4. *Individuals involved in due process hearings should be provided with background information on laws relevant to the issues involved.* When formal due process procedures are invoked, specific and often sophisticated legal concepts may be involved. The fields of sexual discrimination and harassment, discrimination because of disabilities, and affirmative action, to mention only a few, have become increasingly complex over recent years. To fairly evaluate disputed facts in these areas, institutional decision makers must be informed of relevant standards and current interpretations of the law, which can often be accomplished only with the advice of experts. Institutions must commit sufficient resources to obtain qualified counsel when confronted with cases that involve specialized areas of law.

APPENDIX A: A Scenario and Analysis Describing Due Process in Higher Education

The Scenario, Part 1

In his position as assistant dean of students, Dr. Adam Richardson had only limited experience with student hearings under the academic and disciplinary regulations at Wilson State University. In the 11 months since his appointment, he had handled several unrelated instances of plagiarism and an incident in which two freshmen had been caught stealing money from a soft drink machine in their dormitory. Although Richardson was not entirely comfortable with his understanding of the exact requirements of the Wilson State disciplinary code, those cases had been relatively cut and dried and they seemed to dictate their own procedures and penalties. No one had complained about his decisions or the way he had resolved the issues. But the file that was now open on the desk before him had a special and disturbing element: a letter from a lawyer.

Upon first reading, it appeared to Richardson that the lawyer's client, Erica Washington, did not have a leg to stand on. She was challenging the grade of D that she had received from Dr. Steve Ingalls in an undergraduate criminal justice class, CJ-444, Seminar in the Administration of Justice. Because she was already on academic probation, the D brought her grade point average to a level where Washington faced automatic suspension for one academic term.

Being familiar with some of the literature on student rights, Richardson knew that students who challenged grades had an uphill battle. It was Richardson's understanding that the courts were reluctant to second-guess professors when it came to the business of evaluating academic work and awarding grades. Richardson perceived that students were due only limited procedural protection in such cases, certainly less than they would receive in proceedings based on disciplinary complaints. One article he had saved indicated that unless they could show arbitrary or clearly malicious action on the part of a professor, students rarely prevailed in these types of cases. Still, as Richardson considered some of the facts in the matter at hand, he became increasingly concerned.

Ingalls was young and had been on the faculty only two years, but he was well qualified and no complaints from students had previously been received regarding his classes. In response to Richardson's inquiry, the professor had submitted a memorandum describing the basis for Washington's grade. His reasoning was clear. As set out in the course syllabus, the final grade was composed of the student's score on a midterm, a final exam, and an in-class presentation. Washington had scored rather well on the midterm exam, but her low scores on the final and on her presentation left her with only 65 out of a possible 100 points. According to the syllabus, this score translated into a D.

Based on the memorandum and brief discussions of the case with Ingalls and the chair of the Criminal Justice Department, the resolution of the case initially seemed straightforward. But according to Washington, the grade she received was unfair. She contended that the CJ-444 class was dominated by a small group of male students. These students, according to the letter from Washington's attorney, were local police officers whose experience and position apparently impressed Ingalls. At least that was apparent to Washington because, in her opinion, Ingalls allowed this group to use most of each day's class time to tell war stories about their experiences on the street. At the same time, these students took every opportunity to voice the opinion that females were not qualified for police work. According to Washington, these students became personally abusive to her in class each time she tried to defend affirmative action practices in the field of law enforcement. She felt that Ingalls took the side of these students against her, and did not respect her opinion.

The attorney's letter also stated that students in the class would often ridicule Washington's comments and that they frequently made derogatory remarks about female police officers. Washington was said to have protested this treatment, first in class and later privately with Ingalls. According to Washington, Ingalls told her that the discussion of current issues in law enforcement was an important part of the class and that he did not perceive the comments made in class were abusive. Washington later took her complaint to the chair of the Criminal Justice Department but received what she believed was a similar, cursory response. After confirming that none of the comments were of a sexual nature, the chair had suggested that some amount of give-and-take was commonplace with cops and that if she intended to pursue a career in criminal justice, she should learn to forcefully state her opinions and "not be intimidated by a few jokes."

After obtaining what she felt was an unsatisfactory response to her complaints, Washington began to attend class less and less frequently, which, she said, contributed to her low grade on the final exam. She further maintained that she intentionally gave a very short presentation because she did not want to give certain students in the class more of an opportunity to ridicule her position on the hiring of women in law enforcement. She stated that she did not pursue her complaints beyond the chair because, in light of his response, she did not think it would help. Faced with suspension, however, Washington and her attorney now contended that the grade she received was unfair.

After receiving the attorney's letter, Richardson met with Ingalls. The professor stated that after Washington complained about the treatment she received from other students, he did urge the entire class to be more tolerant of each other's opinions. He was adamant, however, that Washington was not the victim of discrimination or sexual harassment and that she received the grade she deserved in the class. He maintained that the class was an upper-level, "seminar-style" class and that an important component of the class included coping strategies and methods of interaction with those who disagreed with a student's views. The chair of the department fully supported Ingalls's position.

As assistant dean, it was Richardson's responsibility to assure that Washington received due process. Her lawyer insisted that Washington was entitled to a hearing and that she, the lawyer, should be given the opportunity to fully participate in the inquiry. Her letter announced her intention to "voir dire" each proposed member of the tribunal that would decide the case, and demanded the right to cross-examine not only Ingalls and the department chair, but also each student in the class. She also demanded copies of each student's midterm and final exam papers and Ingalls's grading notes on the class presentations. The lawyer notified Richardson that at the hearing she would present testimony from two psychologists to describe the impact that the class had had upon Washington as well as what she called the "academic implications of the hostile and abusive atmosphere [that] prevailed in . . . [Ingalls's] class." In closing, the attorney cited a portion of the Wilson State University student handbook that allowed students to file grievances if they felt they had been treated unfairly. The letter formally invoked the grievance procedure on Washington's behalf.

At the request of Wilson State University's attorney, Barbara McCord, Richardson had faxed her the letter from Washington's attorney along with a summary of his conversations with the faculty members involved. He received a fax in return of a chart containing six questions and a handwritten note: "Adam, please consider the three questions under the heading 'substantive due process' on this sheet. I'll call you around nine tomorrow morning."

Analysis. Several issues immediately confront Richardson. This case appears to fall into the category of an "academic challenge" rather than a disciplinary matter—which would initially appear to simplify the legal requirements for due process because under *Board of Curators v. Horowitz* (1978), the Supreme Court recognized that less stringent due process procedures are necessary when academic penalties are imposed. All that initially appears to be at stake is a low grade rather than a more serious disciplinary penalty such as expulsion from the university. But Ingalls may have condoned and ratified the conduct of his students, and if the grade he awarded was influenced by gender-based discrimination, an inquiry into this matter must examine much more than Washington's academic work. In addition to Washington's complaint about her treatment, the issue of academic freedom could be raised by Ingalls if his grading decision is overruled.

Consider whether this case actually involves a factual dispute and whether the university is responsible for the actions of Washington's fellow students. Many of the crucial facts may turn out to be undisputed, but a great deal depends on how the institution officially interprets the agreed-upon facts. The comments by Washington's classmates and the impact they had on her grade must be carefully evaluated. On May 24, 1999, the U. S. Supreme Court ruled in *Davis v. Monroe County Board of Education* that a legal cause of action may be brought under Title IX of the Education Amendments of 1972 (which prohibits sex discrimination in federally supported education) for "student-on-student" harassment. Although the case involved an elementary school student, there is little doubt that the case expands the legal liability of institutions of higher education. Inaction or deliberate indifference by university officials to known harassment can result in awards of damages against the school.

To resolve this complaint, Richardson and Wilson State University will be required to accept one factual interpretation over another. To make this choice, an appropriate inquiry into the content and nature of the comments made during the class is in order. What method should be used to accomplish this inquiry? How detailed must the inquiry be? Richardson observed that some misconduct cases seem to suggest their own proper level of procedural complexity, but others, such as the case at hand, could be handled in a number of very different ways.

The three questions the attorney asked Richardson to consider are those listed under "substantive due process" in Figure 1 on page 38:

- SDP-I. Are applicable university regulations reasonably clear in explaining the kinds of conduct that are required or prohibited and the sanctions that will be imposed if the regulations are violated?
- SDP-II. Is the operation of the applicable university regulations in this case likely to result in a fair decision, one that is neither arbitrary nor capricious?
- SDP-III. Does insurmountable institutional bias exist that precludes internal resolution of this case?

The Scenario, Part 2
Richardson had sent copies of Washington's correspondence, the letter from her attorney, and a summary of the interviews Richardson conducted with Ingalls and the department chair, Dr. Tom Owens, to the university provost, the dean of students, and the university attorney. McCord was true to her word, and Richardson received her call the following morning promptly at 9:00 A.M.

"Barbara, how are you?"

"Fine, thanks, Adam. Yourself?"

"Doing well, but I'm becoming more and more confused with this matter with Ms. Washington."

"That's good. You're doing the right thing so far."

"But not making much progress, I'm afraid."

"Still, you're thinking about it, confronting it, and that's what needs to be done initially. How does it look to you at this point?"

Richardson paused, then said, "I want to make sure we give this student due process, but I hate to get involved in a drawn-out inquiry into who said what over the course of the semester and what it meant. Am I correct in thinking that there was a case that says students have no right to a hearing to challenge a grade?"

"Well, Adam, you're probably thinking of a couple of Supreme Court cases that came out awhile back. In the *Horowitz* case, a medical student was dismissed on academic grounds without a hearing. The student did get an independent evaluation from a group of doctors, but they agreed that she was not qualified to continue in medical school. The Court said she wasn't entitled to a hearing, and that there was no overall substantive due process violation. In other words, she couldn't show that the university acted in an arbitrary or capricious manner."

"So is that the answer for us? We're okay as long as we don't act arbitrarily. . . ."

"It's never that simple, Adam. In fact, the first point I want to impress on you is that there is no single correct answer here. There are any number of ways we can go on this, and only time will tell how correct we were."

Richardson persisted. "But would you say that *generally* these kinds of cases don't require hearings?"

"I wish I could give you a straight yes-or-no answer on that, but the law on due process is rarely clear. I don't think the Supreme Court wants the law in this area to be completely settled."

The attorney continued. "In the mid-80s, there was a case where another medical student was dismissed from the University of Michigan on academic grounds. Even though it appeared that the student had been treated differently from most other medical students, the Court took great pains to safeguard the academic freedom of state universities. Because it appeared to the Court that the faculty made a careful and conscientious decision, their decision was upheld. The Supreme Court held that federal court is simply not the place to evaluate the academic decisions of university faculty."

"That confirms that for an *academic* decision, a student has no right to a hearing. Right?"

"Sorry, Adam, I'm afraid my considered legal opinion is 'it depends.'"

"I thought so. The Court changed its mind, right?"

"Actually, no. Those cases are the Supreme Court's last pronouncements on academic dismissals. No, the problem is that the Court was careful to limit those holdings. Believe me, when it comes to due process, the Court does not set out many concrete rules.

They left open the possibility that protected liberty and property interests *could* exist in academic cases, and stopped short of creating the hard-and-fast policy you're looking for. It is clear that students are entitled to greater due process protection in disciplinary actions than in academic decision making, but where there are allegations of 'bad faith,' courts do require hearings in many so-called 'academic challenge' cases, so there is just no definitive word."

"Great. Then how do we sort this out?"

"One step at a time. I faxed you six questions that I think can guide us through most due process cases. Have you had a chance to look them over?"

"Yes. I think I understand the first three, which deal with substantive due process. Number one asks whether our regulations are clear. I reviewed the WSU academic code, which is part of the student handbook. In answer to that question, I would have to say that the code spells out the required grade point average in no uncertain terms. According to the code, Ms. Washington should be automatically suspended, but I also reexamined our student grievance procedure. It is clear on its face, but then I thought about the second question you sent. Is the actual operation of the rules and regulations going to be fair in this case? I'm not so sure that the combination of the academic code and the grievance procedure are going to result in a fair outcome if they are strictly applied. And I'm not sure how to remedy the problem."

"I have the same misgivings, so let's break it down. Begin with where this is in the system," responded McCord. "All that has really occurred is that Ms. Washington, through her counsel, has notified us of a grievance, and she hasn't really done that properly. The handbook says a student who has a problem with a professor is to proceed up the chain of command to the department chair, then to the dean of the college in which the department is located, and only then to your office. She has actually bypassed the dean of the College of Arts and Sciences, directing her grievance to you."

"So do we send it back down?"

"We could, but in this case I think we should let that slide. While it's important that the procedure be followed, there is a crucial time factor in this case. I don't think we should elevate form over substance. And we are now on notice that student-on-student harassment may have occurred, and it becomes our responsibility to investigate that possibility. At this point, you can handle it like any other grievance."

"That sounds good, but as far as I can tell we don't really have a specific *hearing* procedure for a grievance. The handbook's grievance procedure says due process will be provided but doesn't explain what that means. It doesn't say whether students can have a lawyer or whether they can do all the things Ms. Washington's attorney is demanding."

"Right, and some people might disagree with me, but in my opinion that's all our code needs to say. We need to consider Ms. Washington's claims and decide what procedures will amount to due process in this particular instance."

"But isn't that a question for the courts? I mean, her attorney is obviously thinking in terms of a complex and lengthy hearing. If we don't provide what she wants, isn't she going to claim a denial of due process?"

"She may, Adam. And we may have to defend in court the procedure we choose to provide. That's always a possibility. But we can't let her attorney dictate the structure and content of due process in this case. That has to be our decision."

"Well, if she's going to have her attorney there, I know that we will want you to handle our side."

"Whoa, Adam. We haven't decided if we're going to allow her to even attend the hearing, much less the extent to which she can participate if she's there."

"Yes. I just want to be absolutely certain that we provide the due process that a court would say Ms. Washington is entitled to. Is that possible?"

"Sure. We could be absolutely safe by going out and hiring a retired judge to hear the case, let Ms. Washington's attorney engage in full legal discovery before the hearing, and then essentially conduct a full-scale civil trial. The only problems are that all that process would take months or years to accomplish, and the cost would be enormous."

"But isn't that what a judge would require?"

"Not at all. Judges realize what you're up against here. Wilson State's job is to educate students, not conduct trials. If this lands in court, a judge is going to expect you to have acted in a fair and reasonable manner, to decide the case in good faith. That's the bottom line."

"Okay, that sounds good, but we still have to decide how to proceed."

"True, so let's return to the questions we started to answer. I think they can steer us in the right direction. If I understand you correctly, you feel that the regulations on academic suspension and grievances are clear, in and of themselves, but they don't seem to fit the particular circumstances we have here."

"Exactly. I would answer the first one, SDP-I, affirmatively. The rule seems a bit harsh to me, but it is clear. Ms. Washington was on notice that if her grade point average fell below 2.0, she would be suspended. Our grievance procedure also seems logical and sufficient for its purpose."

"Alright, as to the second question, SDP-II, you feel the regulations may not result in a fair outcome in this particular case?"

"Right. Normally, if a student challenged a professor's academic evaluation, I would simply check the *calculation* of her grade against the course syllabus, but I wouldn't look behind the scores. That would interfere with the professor's academic freedom."

"Perhaps."

"I'm not going to regrade students' papers every time they disagree with their professors' analyses."

"And Ms. Washington is asking for even more than that."

Richardson nodded. "She wants us to look behind her grade, at the reasons for her low score. I don't think our policies ever envisioned that."

"It is highly unusual. So if the policy is clear, explain to me why you are troubled in this case."

"Well, because underlying her complaint is the possibility of discrimination or some kind of harassment. If we just go by the letter of the law, or the letter of our regulations, that possibility will not be explored. That troubles me."

"Adam, I think you have an accurate understanding of the issues here. If you're suggesting that we need to disregard the regulations to some extent, for the sake of fairness and to investigate possible harassment, I agree with you."

Richardson paused, then said, "I didn't realize that was my suggestion, but I suppose it is. I'm reluctant because I'm not sure what it means in practical terms."

"That's what we can figure out when we come to procedural due process, the latter three questions on the document I sent. But there is one last substantive due process concern: the question marked SDP-III."

"The one about insurmountable bias."

"Right. We can go into this inquiry in more depth when we decide who should hear this case, but it's important to explore the possibility of institutional bias from the outset."

Richardson asked, "Can you clarify what's meant by 'institutional bias' here? I understand that the university should approach Ms. Washington's grievance with impartiality, but to me that goes without saying."

"This is another safeguard against arbitrary and capricious decision making. In some cases, a school could be so invested in one position, so protective of its own interests, that it simply could not offer a fair hearing. This is an extreme case, but suppose a college president was alleged to have sexually harassed a student. Or say a professor alleged that a trustee of the university was improperly recruiting student athletes. When the damage that could be done to a school's reputation or finances is so severe that its objectivity is apparently compromised, an internal proceeding may not be appropriate."

"I see. But while I hate to think that the kind of discrimination Ms. Washington is alleging might actually have occurred, I do think that I can be fair. And I think that the administration of Wilson State can be objective in this case."

"That's fine, Adam. As I said, we can return to the question of bias when we consider who should be the hearing officer in this case, but for now I feel comfortable with our efforts toward substantive due process."

Analysis. The essence of substantive due process is a decision based on a scrupulous analysis of the relevant facts in a case rather than an analysis tainted by bias or capriciousness. Richardson has considered the potential in this situation that an unfair decision might be made. He confirmed that Washington was properly on notice of potential adverse action against her by Wilson State University in that the applicable regulations were clear. Then, by examining the actual operation of those regulations and potential bias within the administrative decision-making mechanism, Richardson reduced the possibility that the university's action will be arbitrary or capricious. Thus, the groundwork for substantive due process has been laid. As will be seen, however, the requirements of substantive and procedural due process intersect at crucial points as the case proceeds.

The Scenario, Part 3

After McCord, Wilson State University's counsel, discussed the requirements of substantive due process with Richardson, she explained how they would decide which procedural safeguards would be offered as the student's grievance was heard. She continued to use the diagram they had previously consulted. With respect to procedural due process, McCall urged Richardson to consider the nature of the grievance brought by Washington, the student.

"You first need to decide the overall level of procedural formality appropriate for this case. We've already started on that by discussing the fact that the handbook and other university policies don't require any particular procedures and that this case can be characterized as academic, rather than disciplinary."

Richardson responded, "That would tend to make it less formal then?"

"Right," said the attorney, "but part of Ms. Washington's grievance involves discrimination or harassment, rather than a purely academic challenge."

"True, but that's not clear to me. Shouldn't she be required to state exactly what her problem is before we can address it?"

"You could take that position. Especially since she has a lawyer." After a moment, McCord continued, "We could get into a lot of procedural arguments, Adam. But let's remember that judge who might be looking at this thing down the road and see whether we can cut to the chase. We know what Ms. Washington's problem is. She's saying she got a low grade not because she deserved it but because of harassment or discrimination. The professor and the department chair disagree with her. The university has to take one side or the other."

"Agreed. And we need to investigate what happened so that we will be able to take a position."

"Exactly. Now that investigation will be by way of a hearing. The question now is the appropriate depth of the procedure required at that hearing. We begin with the expectation that this case will not involve many facts that are in dispute. I don't think either side will try to misstate the facts. . . ."

Richardson nodded. "I think I see where you're going. This isn't a case where the skills of a lawyer are really necessary. I mean she could probably state Washington's arguments more clearly, but she is not really needed to bring out the facts in this case."

"Yes. There are some cases where the need for cross-examination by a lawyer is crucial, but this does not seem to be one of them. But you're getting a little ahead of me, Adam. Before we look at these kinds of procedural safeguards specifically, let's focus on the larger picture. We need to get some kind of feel for the level of complexity appropriate for this case as it travels through our system. We need to decide how we're going to handle her case through the steps of notice, hearing, and appeal. More important, you will have to make numerous decisions throughout the process, and to do that you need to have a fairly clear idea of the level of procedure that this case needs. Once you have that, the specific decisions will be easier."

"Okay, I believe I understand what you mean about the level of procedural complexity, but I'm not sure I understand the first choice I'm supposed to make. Isn't the procedure for the hearing something that should be set by university policy?"

"That's a good question, and in theory that's perhaps how it should be. Sometimes the regulations or the faculty or student handbook will clearly spell out what steps to take. But more often, as you know, the handbook just makes a general statement. Our student handbook simply says that due process will be provided in these kinds of cases; it doesn't explain what that means. In this case, I see no reason to proceed in a manner that's highly legalistic. If you recall from the information I sent you, the 'litigation model' is intended for cases where there's no hope for reconciliation and the university intends to prepare for future litigation."

Richardson shook his head slowly. "Right. I hope it won't come to that, but at this point I'm not feeling terribly optimistic. If we rule out the 'litigation model,' the choice is between an 'adversarial model' and an 'informal model?'"

"Yes. First examine the nature of this case. What's at stake? What does Ms. Washington stand to lose here?"

"That's part of what bothers me. From Dr. Ingalls's perspective, all that's in dispute is the grade of D that he gave her. She says she deserves a higher grade; he says she does not. So all that's really in dispute is a letter grade or two. But it just happens that Ms. Washington was already on academic probation and the grade of D automatically puts her out of school for a semester."

"Exactly. So the question is, what *is* at issue? Is it just a matter of a letter grade or is it that harassment or gender discrimination threatens Ms. Washington's educational opportunity at a public institution?"

Richardson paused. "Barbara, I guess that's the problem for me. I'm not sure."

"You could go either way on it, Adam."

"I appreciate that the decision is ultimately mine, well, ultimately that of Wilson State, but I'd like to know your opinion."

"Sure. I feel the bottom line is the fact that she will be out of school if the grade stands. Dr. Ingalls will disagree, but I'd have to say that the nature of this case involves a deprivation more serious than a letter grade."

"And that argues in favor of a higher level of procedural complexity, right?"

"Yes, and other factors also come into play."

"The discrimination claim." Richardson began to make notes on the legal pad before him as he spoke. "Let me see if I understand. She says the class involved harassment based on gender. If not for that, I would be much more comfortable with an informal approach. These grade disputes are bound to come up frequently. I don't like setting the precedent that we will have a complicated hearing every time a student disagrees with his grade."

"Agreed. If you set a procedural format precedent in several cases of the same type, you may be stuck with it in the future. So we can say that the implied allegation of discrimination does complicate matters, but the question is whether that allegation and the penalty involved are enough to require the more formal, or 'adversarial' approach."

"To tell you the truth, Barbara, I'm still not sure."

"Okay, let's think of it this way. What's it going to take to get to the truth here? In order to decide if there was discrimination or if the grade was fair in this case, do you see yourself being more effective in the role of a judge in a court case, or would you have a better chance to get at the truth if you took a more active role in the process?"

"More active? I'm not sure I understand what you mean by that. Such as what?"

"Questioning the witnesses yourself, deciding for yourself when you've heard enough, rather than letting the parties decide when they're finished. Perhaps calling in witnesses on your own or excluding repetitive witnesses. That sort of thing."

"Yes. It seems to me that would be better in this case."

"Okay."

"But isn't that always going to be the case? I mean, I don't ever want to have to sit through a lot of legalistic questioning when I could do it more efficiently myself. . . ."

"Not necessarily, Adam. Imagine a case where there are more disputed facts than we have before us now. Do you remember the case where a student was charged with what the university defined as 'sexual misconduct' after he had relations with a female student who later said she was drunk?"

"Yes. As I recall it, there were issues about who did what, but it was basically her word against his. A difficult case."

"Exactly, and I'll bet you would not be so comfortable with an informal procedure if you had to decide a case like that."

"True enough. I would want both sides to feel that they were able to say whatever it was they wanted to say."

"Same situation in some cheating cases, where the evidence is hotly disputed. There is room for even some of what you might call 'useless' questioning in these cases just for the sake of completeness and maybe also for the psychological benefit that comes from allowing everyone to have his or her say. Remember what I said about hard-and-fast rules, Adam. There are none when it comes to due process in higher education. An allegation of cheating on a test is not the same, I think, as a case of garden variety plagiarism. Both are academic misconduct cases, but you might want to approach them with different levels of procedural complexity."

"Okay. I'm beginning to see what you mean. It comes down to the nature and circumstances of each individual case."

Analysis. With respect to the requirements of due process, no single perfect hearing format exists. Unless a school's policies are explicit, a number of decisions about procedure must be made. The same case may be addressed, correctly, in a number of different ways through the use of different combinations of procedural safeguards. Rather than trying to force a particular hearing procedure to fit a particular *type* of case, it is better to consider the individual due process protection required by the nature of each case. Richardson has come to recognize that while this case may appear to be a simple grade challenge, the issues are more complicated than in "typical" academic challenge cases.

In determining the proper procedure for any given case, an administrator should always begin with the policies and regulations published by his or her particular institution. Even if those regulations call for more protection than appears to be required by the nature of the case, the procedures promised in the regulations should nonetheless be followed. But if institutional regulations call for less protection than appears warranted in a particular case, the administrator should supplement the prescribed procedure with whatever additional safeguards he or she finds to be appropriate in keeping with the nature and facts of the case.

Although it may be possible to consistently meet the requirements of constitutional due process by adopting a formal and highly legalistic model of procedure, this approach is neither economical nor efficient. Richardson chose a course of action somewhere between an informal discussion and an adversarial hearing. Had the dispute involved only the letter grade, he could have chosen to discuss informally the issues with the parties. He would still have considered a range of procedural safeguards, but the inquiry could have been streamlined. He would still have provided Washington with the opportunity to present her case, only in less depth, with fewer procedural rights than she will be provided under a more adversarial approach.

Richardson's discussion with the university attorney has been productive. Instead of allowing Washington's attorney to dictate the requirements of due process in this case, Richardson understands that decisions about the way the hearing in this case is conducted remain with the university. With that power to choose comes the responsibility to act fairly and reasonably. Ultimately, his choices may be scrutinized by a judge (or judges), and although his judgment will be given deference, the process actually provided to Washington must not fall below the standard of due process to which she is constitutionally entitled.

The Scenario, Part 4

McCord discussed the general parameters of Washington's case with Richardson, covering some of the legal background on the thorny relationship among academic freedom, freedom of speech, and allegations of harassment. She suggested that it was time to begin making practical decisions that would determine the nature and extent of the hearing to be held in the case.

"The hard question in this case is who will make the decision," said McCord. "Is it going to be you, or an independent hearing officer, or perhaps a hearing panel composed of students and faculty members?"

"That is a tough one. I don't suppose the handbook tells us."

"Afraid not, but you're wise to consider that possibility first. In some situations, for example, in tenure disputes at Wilson State, our policy *does* spell out who hears the case and describes some of the required procedures. The school's written policies or even its established customs should always be consulted first. But in this case you are going to have to make the decision without that guidance."

"Then I'm lost again, Barbara. I can see some justification for having a panel decide this issue, but on the other hand, I honestly think I could be fair. I just don't know."

"You may be closer than you think, Adam. You said you *honestly* felt you could be fair. That was going to be my next question to you: Do you have any bias that you're aware of that would color your decision in this case? What I'm trying to suggest is that you need to honestly examine Wilson State's position and your own position here, and decide whether it's fair for you to proceed as the person who handles this case."

"What if I feel I could not be fair?"

"Then we would need to locate someone either with the school or independent from Wilson State who can."

"I don't think I have any bias in this case, but it's possible that I might lean in favor of Dr. Ingalls over the student. I mean, in any case, I'd hate to see a professor in the wrong. It will be much easier if Ms. Washington is found to deserve the grade she got."

"Don't misunderstand me, Adam. I'm not asking for a psychological evaluation of your unconscious mind. All I'm asking is whether you can say in good faith that you would decide the case based on the evidence you hear rather than on your feelings about what might be best for your employer or for you."

"I believe I can be objective. I'll try to be, but maybe I should point out that Dr. Owens, the chair of the Criminal Justice Department, was on the search committee that hired me as assistant dean."

"Oh, I didn't know that, but that is another factor to be taken into consideration. I'm not questioning your ability to be objective, but we do have to bear in mind that a judge may look at this situation someday and be realistic. If there is the appearance of impropriety, that appearance is going to have to be explained if the case should ever go to court. Even if you are sure that your relationship with Dr. Owens will not affect your judgment and you could testify to that under oath, it's still a factor to consider in making this decision."

"Well, if we make this decision in terms of relationships, I'll probably never decide a case because I know just about all the professors on campus. I've served on committees with many of them."

"I understand what you're saying, Adam. And the courts recognize that university communities are often relatively small. That doesn't rule out your decision making in these cases. It's just one more factor to take into account. It does seem to me that the fact that Dr. Owens was directly involved in hiring you is substantially different from simply serving together on a committee."

"Okay. I suppose it might be best here to appoint someone else. But I think it should be one person, not a panel."

"Agreed. Now, suppose you're under oath and I'm a judge. Tell me why."

"Because of all the things we've been talking about. Assembling a panel of decision makers would complicate this matter quite a bit. It does not appear that the facts are going to be seriously contested. So a single objective person can judge whether there was discrimination in the class just as well as a group could. Having more than one decision maker is not more likely to lead to an accurate decision."

"Excellent, Adam. You've just engaged in a 'balancing analysis.' You looked at the interests on both sides and the extent to which the use of a panel would increase the chances of getting at the truth. And I think you are demonstrating the kind of 'good faith' that a court would be looking for, if it ever comes to that. Do you have someone in mind for the job?"

"You've given me such a hard time that I'd like to appoint you, but I guess I can't do that."

"An interesting idea, but I would have to decline."

"Thought so. One person I can suggest is Dr. Anna Jennings in the Physical Sciences Department. She has been teaching at Wilson for almost 20 years, and most of the faculty and students know her to be a fair and independent professor."

"Okay, but before you make the decision, remember the balancing test. Do you think it might be necessary in this case to allow Ms. Washington to participate in the decision as to who hears this case?"

"I can see where she would *want* to name the hearing officer; in fact, I suppose she might want us to use the option of a hearing panel, with students on it, to make the decision here. But I don't believe the circumstances here would justify the time and extra trouble that would involve. As I said, I don't expect that the facts will be seriously in dispute. It seems to me that one fair person can make this decision as well as a group could."

"That's fine then. I believe you're on solid ground legally and in terms of the fair resolution of this grievance. You've made some of the hard decisions, but let's take a break. When we get back together, I'd like to return to the issue of bias. At this point, I want you to consider bias in terms of the procedural due process decision about a hearing officer."

"I thought that was a substantive due process issue."

"This is a point where substance and procedure intertwine. I want you to return to those factors that might influence you or the university. I'm not talking about the *appearance* of good faith here; I'm looking for some real soul-searching, and let me tell you why I ask. Well, first because it's the right thing to do, to identify any possible bias, but beyond that, let's suppose this matter does go to court someday. Some lawyers and judges, and some jurors for that matter, are quite good at evaluating when a witness is uncomfortable about his testimony. Even when a person is not lying but is just not telling everything, a lawyer's antennae go up."

When Richardson raised his eyebrows, McCord continued, "Please, Adam, no lawyer jokes comparing us to insects. What I'm saying is, if you haven't confronted all the possible bias and dealt with it in a straightforward manner, it's going to affect you in some way on the witness stand. I want us to lay all the cards on the table right now. We need to acknowledge and confront any bias that may exist."

"I have no problem with that, but I'm just not sure whether, or to what extent, there may be bias, personally or on behalf of the university."

"I'd like for us to get together after lunch and discuss it. Between now and then, just think about it. . . ."

Analysis. The question as to who should decide the Washington case requires Richardson to confront subjective issues as to his involvement and the involvement of the university in hearing the case. On rare occasions, there may be cases where the interests of the school, or a particular administrator, may be so weighted toward a particular outcome that the case must be referred to decision makers outside the institution. Richardson must identify not only his actual bias, but also the appearance of bias on his part or with respect to the university as a whole.

As this scenario continues, Richardson makes decisions about the structure of the hearing to be held in this case.

The Scenario, Part 5

Richardson felt that substantial progress had been made, but he realized that many difficult decisions remained before a hearing in Washington's case could proceed. He remained troubled by the possible existence of bias on the part of the university as a whole and in his own mind. That afternoon he met again with McCord in the conference room of the Wilson State University administration building.

The attorney began the discussion with a question. "Well, Adam, have you come to any conclusions about prejudice that might influence this case?"

"I have a few concerns, Barbara. The first issue is the fact that if Ms. Washington is ruled to be correct in what she says, that means that Dr. Ingalls engaged in discrimination. That doesn't look good for the university, and I expect that Dr. Ingalls will strongly disagree. He is taking these accusations personally, and I can't blame him. So to that extent, it becomes a somewhat personal issue for me. Beyond that, I expect that many faculty members would perceive this as an attack on academic freedom. That's always a sensitive issue, and I expect that both the university as a whole and I, personally, would be relieved if Ms. Washington's allegations were determined to be unfounded."

"Okay, Adam. That strikes me as an honest assessment. There is also the difficult issue of the right of the students in the class to freedom of speech. But the immediate question is whether those feelings will prevent a fair hearing from taking place."

"I've given that further thought also, Barbara, and as I indicated earlier, I don't think the pressures in this case are so great that they would interfere with my carrying out the responsibility to be fair. It seems to me that in almost every case there are going to be similar problems. You could say that I have some bias, but in this case I believe the pressure is manageable."

"That's what I needed to hear, Adam. I think we're ready to move on. We need to look now at the depth of procedural protection that is justified by the seriousness of the case and our need for an efficient resolution."

"Right. Where do we begin?"

"Let's start with the question of an open hearing. Unless you know of some reason why this matter should be open to the university community, I recommend that it be closed except to the extent Ms. Washington wants to invite others. Because it involves Ms. Washington's grades, it might violate federal laws to make the hearing public."

"Fine with me. What's next?"

"The issue of discovery. Are there any documents in our possession or in Dr. Ingalls's possession that Ms. Washington may need, whether she is aware of them or not?"

"I can't think of anything."

"Any objection to providing her any documents she asks for? I mean within reason."

"No problem, as far as I know."

"Well, then, let's decide who should testify at the hearing. . . ."

Consulting Washington's original letter as well as notes taken from earlier conversations with Ingalls and the class roster, Richardson and McCord identified several students from the class who, along with Ingalls, would be able to provide important testimony. They discussed whether other class members should be requested or required to submit written statements. McCord suggested that this procedure might be justified after balancing the interests. Richardson decided that the hearing officer would need to hear live testimony to understand what happened in the class. He felt that Jennings might need to explore the context of certain statements and events that would be discussed. They also decided that Washington would not be offered an opportunity to take any written statements or depositions before the hearing and that no further investigation was necessary before scheduling the hearing date.

Richardson and McCord then considered the procedural safeguards that would be appropriate during the hearing. The decision to tape-record the hearing rather than simply keeping notes was made quickly, but more difficult decisions were required when they discussed the procedure by which evidence would be heard. Their discussion led to questions about the extent to which Washington's attorney would participate in the hearing. Richardson questioned whether it was even possible to decide at this time how the hearing would proceed in light of the many potential problems that might emerge during the course of the hearing.

The attorney explained that the purpose of their current discussion was primarily to prepare the notice that would be sent to Washington. It would be a letter setting the hearing date and generally describing the way the hearing would proceed. "All we have to do is formulate a fairly clear picture of how the hearing should proceed," said McCord. "Once the hearing begins, you may decide that you need to provide additional safeguards for Ms. Washington, and you can certainly do that if necessary."

Richardson indicated his concern that the hearing might turn into an unmanageable proceeding. "I would prefer to handle this matter less formally than a court case where attorneys present evidence and object to testimony on technical grounds. I think we can get to the heart of the matter without all that."

"Right. Your view of this case as requiring procedures less complex than under a litigation model implies that attorneys will not present the cases. But what about having them present for consultation?"

"I suppose that would be all right, even though I think it will slow things down."

"It will. So let me hear the reasons why you feel it might be necessary to allow Ms. Washington's attorney to consult with her during the hearing."

"I don't know. I suppose it just seems like we're covering something up if we don't allow the lawyer in."

"Well, what if we allow her to be present, to observe, but not to consult with her client during the hearing?"

"Actually, that seems preferable to me, but can we do that? It seems like some sort of violation, free speech or free association, something along those lines."

"Adam, I'm glad you're sensitized to potential constitutional violations, but remember, this is not a criminal trial. We have to proceed in the way we believe is most appropriate. We may have to justify our decisions before a judge someday, and the judge will decide if we were correct in our assessment of the demands of due process. But in this particular case, we don't even have to allow her attorney in the room if we decide, on balance, that her presence will not significantly add to the likelihood that the decision in the case will be correct."

Richardson and McCord continued to discuss the appropriate role of the attorney in this case and other procedural safeguards over the next hour. Eventually, they arrived at conclusions about both the hearing and the appeal, and were able to prepare the following letter notifying Washington as to the procedures that would be followed during the hearing in her case:

WILSON STATE UNIVERSITY

April 14, 1997

Ms. Anne Erica Washington
Room 456, Wetherford Hall

Wilson State University
—Hand Delivery—

Re: WSU File 789W.121

Dear Ms. Washington,

With reference to your letter to me dated April 3, 1997, and that of your attorney, Ms. Jane Paxton, dated April 7, 1997, please be advised that on May 5, 1997, at 9:00 A.M. in Room 224 of the Wilson University Administration Building, a hearing will be convened to examine your complaint about your grade in CJ-444, Administration of Justice. This hearing will continue throughout the day on May 5, and if necessary we will reconvene the hearing on May 6, 1997, at 9:00 A.M. Your complaint is being treated as a grievance under Section 33.543, on page 30 of the 1996-97 Wilson State University Student Handbook. It is necessary that you be present throughout the hearing in order for your grievance to be addressed. The hearing will be conducted in accordance with the policy statements on pages 30-32 of the Student Handbook. At this point, I am taking the position that this hearing will not be open to the general public or members of the university community; if you would like the hearing to be "open" rather than closed, please notify me immediately so that we can discuss this possibility.

This hearing is your opportunity to present evidence relevant in this matter, subject to the rulings of the hearing officer. Your attorney will be allowed to be present at this hearing but will not be allowed to participate. At the discretion of the hearing officer and during breaks, you will be allowed to consult with your attorney during the hearing; otherwise, however, your attorney's role at this hearing will be limited to observation only. Wilson State University will not be represented by an attorney at this hearing.

The hearing officer will be Dr. Anna Jennings, a member of the faculty of the Physical Sciences Department at Wilson State University. I will initially present evidence relevant to this matter to Dr. Jen-
nings, and following my presentation, you will have the opportunity to call witnesses and ask questions. Dr. Jennings will listen to the evidence presented and to any statement you wish to make, and will render a written hearing decision based solely on the testimony at the hearing within one week of the conclusion of the hearing.

The issues to be decided by Dr. Jennings at the hearing are whether you were subjected to unfair treatment in the CJ-444 class and, if so, whether that treatment resulted in your receiving an unfair grade in the course. Dr. Jennings will also be asked to investigate whether harassment occurred in the class and to make recommendations for further action if she finds affirmatively.

All witnesses who testify at the hearing will be under oath, and the witnesses will not be allowed in the hearing room except during the time they testify. The witnesses whose testimony I intend to present at the Hearing include:

1. Dr. Steve Ingalls, who is expected to testify that the grade you received in CJ-444 was fair and was based solely on your academic performance in the class. You should be aware that during his testimony, Dr. Ingalls will be discussing your academic performance and your grade. This information will therefore be heard by those present during this closed hearing.
2. Mr. Jeremy Alston, who is expected to testify that he was a student in CJ-444, and that you were treated in a reasonable manner in the class and apparently subjected to the same grading criteria as everyone else in the class.
3. Mr. Bob Shields, who is expected to testify that he was a student in CJ-444 and that the treatment you received in the class was substantially the same as that received by each of the other students in the class.

Following my questioning of these witnesses, you may ask them questions if you wish. Also, I will ask you to explain why you feel your grade was unfair. Following any statement you choose to make, or if you make no statement, I may ask you questions about what happened in the CJ-444 class.

At the hearing, you will have the opportunity to call a reasonable number of witnesses, if you wish, to describe what happened in this class. I may ask them questions after they answer your questions. Please notify me in writing at least three days prior to the hearing (no later than May 3, 1997) as to the names of any witnesses you plan to call at the hearing and what you expect them to say. If you fail to notify me in advance as to your witnesses, Dr. Jennings may not allow them to testify. If you need assistance in arranging for the testimony of any member of the university community, please notify me as soon as possible (and in no event no later than May 3, 1997). All witnesses at the hearing will testify at the discretion of the hearing officer, Dr. Jennings, and she may choose to place time limits on the testimony of any witness.

You will also have the opportunity at the hearing to present any documents you feel are relevant to this matter to Dr. Jennings. If there are documents you feel are important to your case that are unavailable to you and are in the possession of Wilson State University or its employees (including Dr. Ingalls), it is important that you notify me immediately (and in no event no later than May 3, 1997).

If you disagree with the written hearing decision issued by Dr. Jennings in this matter, you may request an appeal of her decision by notifying the provost of Wilson State University (Ms. Mary Davis, 200 Wilson Administrative Building) in writing within one week of the date you receive the hearing decision. The subsequent decision by the provost will be the final administrative decision by Wilson State University.

If you have any questions concerning the hearing in your case or wish to discuss it further, please contact me at 555-0000. Based on our previous conversations and the request in your attorney's letter, I will continue to notify you of developments in this case by calling you at 555-1111 or by delivering written notice (with a copy mailed to your attorney) to your dormitory mailbox in Wetherford Hall. If for any reason you cannot be reached in this manner, it is important that you notify me immediately.

In conclusion, I solicit your assistance, and that of your attorney, in conducting a fair and efficient hearing in this matter.

Sincerely,

Adam Richardson, Ph.D.
Assistant Dean
Office of Student Affairs

cc: Ms. Jane Paxton
Attorney at Law

Analysis. Fundamentally, Washington's case remains a dispute about academic evaluation. Were it not for the facts that Washington's grievance involved elements of harassment and gender discrimination and that the potential penalty in her case would be enhanced because of previous academic shortcomings, Richardson undoubtedly would have greatly curtailed the procedural complexity of the hearing in this case. As it is, his decisions to limit the participation of Washington's lawyer, to limit the number of witnesses, and to streamline the appeal process are justified by the circumstances, and should be upheld as reasonable if the case is eventually taken to litigation.

In deciding how a hearing will actually be conducted, it is important for an administrator not only to consider individual procedural safeguards, but also to do so in the context of the entire proceeding. While it may be necessary during the hearing to modify the depth of the procedural safeguards provided (as evidence develops, for example, unexpected witnesses may need to be called, opportunities for cross-examination may need to be expanded, or the degree to which the hearing officer becomes involved may change), the overall nature of the case must determine the procedural complexity of the hearing.

Although Washington did not specifically raise the issue of student-on-student harassment, Wilson State University is on notice that such harassment may have occurred. The hearing in Washington's case provides an opportunity to investigate, and Richardson has asked the hearing officer to make recommendations for further action if she concludes that harassment did occur. Even if a student does not specifically complain, the Supreme Court decision in *Davis v. Monroe County Board of Education,* mentioned earlier, makes it clear that schools must affirmatively address student-on-student harassment.

The Scenario, Part 6
Wilson State University—Case Number 789W.121
In The Matter of Anne Erica Washington (477-99-1818)

Hearing Decision
This case was referred to me as hearing officer by Dr. Adam Richardson, assistant dean in the Wilson State University Office of Student Affairs, on April 23, 1997. It involves a grievance filed by Ms. Erica Washington related to the grade she received during the winter 1997 term in CJ-444, The Administration of Justice, taught by Assistant Professor Dr. Steve Ingalls. Testimony in this matter was presented on May 5 and 6, 1997, in Room 224 of the Wilson University Administration Building. This hearing was not open to the public.

Present at the hearing were Ms. Washington and her attorney, Ms. Jane Paxton (who observed but did not participate in the hearing); Dr. Adam Richardson (who presented witnesses on behalf of Wilson State University); and Dr. Steve Ingalls. The witnesses who testified, in order of their appearance, were Ms. Washington, Dr. Ingalls, Ms. Ruth Wood (a student in the class who was called to testify by Ms. Washington), Dr. Tom Owens (chair of the Department of Criminal Justice, who was called by agreement of both sides), Mr. Jeremy Alston and Mr. Robert Shields (both of whom are students in the class called to testify by Dr. Richardson). Documents accepted during the hearing and considered in rendering this decision were a copy of the class syllabus for CJ-444 and a copy of a page from Dr. Ingalls's grade book (with all names other than Ms. Washington's obscured). I also consulted Wilson State University's published regulations.

Prior to the presentation of testimony I explained (in accordance with instructions from Dr. Richardson) that the hearing would be closed to the public, that I would decide the case based only on evidence presented at the hearing, that Ms. Washington had the burden of establishing that her grade was unfair but that I would decide the case based on the preponderance of the evidence (in other words, the decision would be rendered in favor of whichever side presented the most convincing evidence, even if the difference were slight), that I would render a written hearing decision that included specific findings of fact that supported my decision, and that appeal rights would be set out in my hearing decision.

A tape recording of this hearing was made but has not been transcribed. The tape is in the possession of Dr. Richardson.

Hearing Issues

As formulated by Dr. Richardson prior to the hearing, the hearing issues to be decided are:

1. Was Ms. Washington's grade in CJ-444 unfairly affected by the treatment (specifically the repeated challenging of her opinions by other students) she received in the class?
2. If so, what remedy is appropriate?
3. Did harassment of Ms. Washington occur in the CJ-444 class?
4. If so, what further action is recommended?

Findings of Fact

1. Ms. Erica Washington is a junior, majoring in criminal justice at Wilson State University. She was on academic probation at the beginning of the winter 1997 term, meaning that if her grade point average for the term was less than 3.0 (on a 4.0 point scale), she would automatically be suspended from Wilson State University for the following term.
2. Ms. Washington was enrolled in Dr. Ingalls's CJ-444 Administration of Justice class for the winter 1997 term. In addition to Ms. Washington, 30 other students were enrolled in

this class. Twenty-one of these students were males, and nine of these students, in addition to Ms. Washington, were females.

3. According to Dr. Ingalls's syllabus for CJ-444, each student's grade was determined by adding four scores received during the course: (a) the midterm exam score (30% of the final grade); (b) the final exam score (30% of the final grade); (c) the score on the student's in-class presentation (30% of the final grade); and (d) the score on the student's class participation (10% of the final grade).

4. Ms. Washington received 26 of 30 possible points on the midterm exam, 20 of 30 possible points on the final exam, 17 of 30 possible points on her class presentation, and 4 of 10 possible points for her class participation. She therefore received 67 out of a possible 100 points, resulting in her receiving a letter grade of D in the class.

5. In other classes during the winter 1997 term, Ms. Washington received one grade of A, one grade of B, and one grade of C. With her grade of D in CJ-444, her GPA for the winter 1997 term was less than 3.0, and she was suspended for the spring 1997 term, which begins on May 16, 1997 (six days from the date of this decision).

6. There was dispute in the testimony as to the extent to which Ms. Washington participated in class. I accept the evidence from Dr. Ingalls that Ms. Washington's participation in class was inadequate, and find that she did not regularly participate in class discussions.

7. There was dispute as to whether or to what extent Ms. Washington was treated with disrespect by fellow students during the CJ-444 class. Ms. Washington and Ms. Wood testified that Ms. Washington was treated with disrespect. Mr. Alston and Mr. Shields testified that she was treated with proper respect. In response to questions by Dr. Richardson, both of these students testified that they were not aware of the emotional impact their comments had upon Ms. Washington, and both expressed regret for the manner in which they expressed their opinions. Dr. Ingalls testified that while he did not believe that Ms. Washington was subjected to sexual harassment or verbal abuse, her views were frequently and sometimes harshly challenged by other students in the class. I find that Ms. Washington's comments were challenged by her classmates more frequently than was the case with other students in the class. I find that on numerous occasions, several of the class members, who are police officers, referred to the fact that the general public does not understand the pressures associated with the law enforcement profession and emphasized their belief that difficulties can arise when law enforcement officers are females. I find that in this context reference was made to "ignorant citizens" and that

in this context Ms. Washington was specifically referred to as "ignorant." I find that Ms. Washington's views were the subject of extraordinary scrutiny by both Dr. Ingalls and her fellow students. I further find that this treatment had a negative effect on Ms. Washington's performance and her grade in the CJ-444 class.

8. Dr. Ingalls testified that he was aware that Ms. Washington was not comfortable with the manner in which the class was conducted but that he believed that a seminar style is appropriate for this class. He further stated that he intends to continue to teach the class using the seminar style in the future. Dr. Ingalls also testified, however, that until he heard Ms. Washington's testimony in this case, he did not realize the extent to which she was affected by the treatment she received from other students in the class.

Decision

1. Ms. Erica Washington's grade in CJ-444 was unfairly affected by the treatment in the class. The responsibility for this problem lies partly with the other students in the class, partly with Dr. Ingalls and Dr. Owens, and partly with Ms. Washington herself because she failed to pursue the matter beyond the departmental level.

2. The appropriate remedy for the situation is for Ms. Washington to repeat CJ-444 next term. Her suspension for next term is to be canceled; however, she will remain on academic probation and must achieve that required GPA or again face automatic suspension. It is my hope and expectation that should Ms. Washington encounter what she perceives to be unfair treatment in the class, she will more clearly communicate with Dr. Ingalls or other officials at Wilson State University to resolve the matter. If problems cannot be satisfactorily resolved at the departmental level, I expect Ms. Washington to contact the dean of the College of Arts and Sciences, and later the provost if necessary, as described in Section 133.88 of the Wilson State University student handbook.

3. Student-on-student harassment occurred in the CJ-444 class.

4. I recommend that during the coming term, when Ms. Washington repeats CJ-444, Ms. Washington's class presentation include a debate with Mr. Robert Shields and Mr. Jeremy Alston on the subject of "affirmative action to increase the number of females officers in law enforcement." In this debate, Mr. Shields and Mr. Alston should argue *in favor of* such affirmative action, and Ms. Washington and another student should argue *against* affirmative action. During the hearing, Mr. Shields and Mr. Alston indicated a willingness to voluntarily participate in such a debate, and if they do participate in

this activity in good faith, I recommend that no further action be taken to address this incident of harassment.

Appeal Rights

Any party to this hearing may appeal this hearing decision to the provost of Wilson State University by delivering a written appeal, specifically stating the basis for disagreement with the hearing decision, to the Office of the Provost, Room 200, Wilson University Administration Building, within 10 calendar days of his or her receipt of this decision. At his discretion, the provost may review the testimony and documents submitted in this case, and may request written or oral testimony or argument from the parties. The decision of the provost will be the final administrative action by Wilson State University in this matter.

Signed:

_____

Dr. Anna Jennings

The Scenario, Part 7

Even with the conclusion of the hearing in Washington's case and the issuance of Jennings's written decision, Richardson's work was not finished. Just after the time for an appeal expired, he received a visit from Ingalls. Ingalls said that he had thought carefully about what he heard at the hearing, and wondered what Richardson thought he could or should have done differently. He explained that he still did not believe Washington was subjected to discrimination but that he had a better understanding of why she felt her grade was unfair. Ingalls reiterated his concern that if Washington intended to pursue a career in law enforcement, she needed to learn how to stand up for herself. His intent in the class, he explained, was not only to impart the content of the textbook, but also to provide students like Washington with a taste of reality. As he put it, the "real world" was a tough place, and part of Washington's criminal justice education involved learning how the real world operates.

Richardson began on a conciliatory note. "I'm glad that you have a broad definition of the word 'education,' Steve. And I agree that in this class it is legitimate to incorporate an appreciation for how the law enforcement profession actually functions. I understand your belief that you properly responded to Ms. Washington's complaint as she presented it to you. It appears that you carefully followed the grading structure set out in the course syllabus. What I'd like for you to see is how the concept of due process can make a difference in the classroom when disputes arise."

"Well, that's part of my problem. I don't see that there was a 'dispute' as such. She didn't do the work. She performed poorly on her exam and in her presentation, so she received a low grade."

"I understand what you're saying, and, believe me, this whole approach takes some careful consideration. I'm just coming to appreciate the idea of due process myself, after some long conversations with our attorney. But let's suppose that during the final exam you caught Ms. Washington obviously cheating. Say you saw her reading from her textbook, which was open beneath her desk. Would you say there was dispute then?"

"Not really. Not if I saw with my own eyes that she was reading from the book."

"So what would you do at that point?"

"Well, if you're talking about due process, I don't think there is anything to be gained by having a hearing in that kind of situation. Nothing she could say could change the facts. I would give her an F on the exam."

"That's the way I would have handled it too, until recently. But my conversations with our attorney, Barbara McCord, have changed my thinking to some extent. I think now that one of the most important applications of due process is in those situations where you believe you already 'know' what the facts are and the correct penalty is clear."

"I understand that you're saying it's important to keep an open mind and listen to the student's side of the story, but, really, what's the point? In the situation you described, or in the situation that actually occurred with Ms. Washington, I knew what the facts were because I saw them with my own eyes."

"Then you don't see any need for due process?"

"It seems to me that due process involves an adversarial confrontation between two relatively equal sides. It is almost dishonest to suggest that I will provide Ms. Washington with due process when I already know what I'm going to do. I think the last thing I ought to do in those circumstances is pretend that some kind of watered-down evidentiary hearing is going to change things."

"Your point is well taken, Steve, but I think you are assuming that due process is effective only in criminal cases. If you're talking about locking someone up or imposing a fine on them, then more extensive due process is in order. But I also think that even watered-down due process is valuable. By that I mean a brief hearing, without protections like an attorney or cross-examination, nonetheless allows for an inquiry into the facts. Now I agree that if you cannot approach the inquiry with a truly open mind, then that bias makes the hearing a waste of time. But if an informal and abbreviated hearing is unbiased, I believe that due process is served, which is valuable and necessary in itself."

"I guess that's where we disagree. I don't see that value in a case like this."

"It has to do both with fairness and with the perception of fairness, which I suppose are two distinct things sometimes. There is research indicating that when people are simply given the opportunity to tell their side of the story and are listened to before a decision is made, it makes a big difference in how they see the outcome. That opportunity may be the most important factor in the perception as to whether the decision was fair. Beyond that, I also believe that a commitment to due process requires that we provide a hearing, at whatever level, before a decision is made."

"But I believe I was fair when I made my decision. It seems to me that if Ms. Washington had put as much energy into the class as she did into her grievance, it would have saved us all a lot of trouble."

"That may be, but let me ask you this. Do you think she learned anything from this experience?"

"Well, one part of me wants to say that she learned to use the law to make up for her failure to do her academic work. But I guess that's a narrow view. I can see that this experience might teach her that under our system of justice there are procedures for appeals from certain decisions and there are limits on power."

"And isn't that also true in law enforcement under our system of justice? I seem to recall you once told me that an important component of your class involved coping strategies and methods of interaction with others. So, in a sense, hasn't this experience been a manifestation of what you intended to teach in the classroom about the administration of justice?"

Ingalls said he would have to think about that.

Analysis. It would be nice if disputes in the real world could be resolved as neatly as in this scenario. In the real world, students are not likely to demonstrate the sensitivity shown by Mr. Shields and Mr. Alston, and professors are sometimes less receptive than Dr. Ingalls to insights offered by university administrators. This scenario is intended to illustrate the complexity of the decision-making process with respect to academic and disciplinary hearings in the university setting and the importance of the Supreme Court's recent decision in *Davis v. Monroe County Board of Education*. What appears on its face to be a simple case actually involves significant constitutional conflicts between a student's right to freedom of speech, Dr. Ingalls's academic freedom, and Ms. Washington's right to substantive and procedural due process. Due process hearings in higher education are opportunities for institutions to investigate not only formal grievances and complaints, but also the circumstances involved in situations where they have only informal knowledge of harassment or discriminatory action. The full implications of the *Davis* decision will not be known until more litigation occurs under Title IX, but it is clear that public institutions of higher education have an affirmative duty to conduct prompt, thorough, and fair investigations into formal and informal complaints of student-on-student harassment.

APPENDIX B: A Student Due Process Challenge

Nash v. Auburn University, 812 F.2d 655 (11th Cir. 1987)

Facts and Administrative Actions

David Nash and Donna Perry were first-year students at the Auburn University School of Veterinary Medicine in 1985 when they were accused of cheating on their final exam in neuroanatomy. During the exam, the two students sat close together, out of their assigned seats for the course. The exam was monitored by five faculty members, all of whom noticed the close contact of the students; several of these faculty members and several students later testified that Perry at times would hold her paper up before her as if she were reading it and that Nash would stare at the paper while she did so.

Professor Buxton, who prepared and graded the test, was aware of the suspicious behavior of these students, and he compared and analyzed their answers. He found a strong similarity between their answers on 6 of 28 questions. The professor then became convinced that Nash and Perry were cheating during the test and had the other faculty members who observed the students examine the answers. These faculty members concurred with Professor Buxton that collusion had occurred between Nash and Perry.

On June 6, 1985, the two students were advised in writing that they were charged with a violation of the Student Honor Code. Specifically, they were told that they would be given "at least 72 hours to prepare a defense for the charge of academic dishonesty, in that while taking examinations during 1984-1985 school year, information was allegedly obtained in an unethical manner." By way of this notice, a hearing was scheduled for June 10 before the Student Board of Ethical Relations.

The students appeared on June 10 with an attorney. The lawyer objected to proceeding with the hearing at that time because, he said, the notice the students received on June 6 was inadequate and too general to advise his clients of the charges against them. He asked for more specific notice and additional time to prepare a defense. The board agreed to provide both.

The following day, the students were given a memorandum stating that they were charged with "giving or receiving assistance or communication between students during the anatomy examination given on or about May 16, 1985." Included in the memorandum was a list of students and faculty members who were expected to testify at the hearing. In accordance with the agreement made with the attorney on the previous evening, a new hearing date was set for the following day, June 12, 1985.

The disciplinary hearing was conducted on that date by the student "chancellor" of the Board of Ethical Relations before a number of student "justices." Nash and Perry were present, with their attorney. There was no attorney for the board. The chancellor over the hearing allowed the attorney to advise Nash and Perry during the hearing but not to participate otherwise. Nash and Perry were allowed to indirectly question the witnesses who testified against them; they directed their questions to the chancellor, who then posed questions to the witnesses. Nash and Perry objected to this method of cross-examination, but the student chancellor would not change the established procedure. The hearing was tape-recorded.

After hearing statements from the faculty and students supporting the charge of academic misconduct, Nash and Perry were allowed to make their own statements; they denied that they had cheated. They were also allowed to bring in their own witnesses, other students who were in the exam who stated they did not see any cheating occur. They requested a recess during the hearing, apparently for in-depth consultation with their attorney, but the student chancellor denied this request.

After the testimony was concluded, the board deliberated in private, and decided unanimously that Nash and Perry were guilty of the charge of academic dishonesty. The student justices recommended that they be suspended with the opportunity to reapply for admission in one year. Nash and Perry were notified of this decision and recommendation and of their right to appeal to the dean of the Auburn University School of Veterinary Medicine. They undertook that appeal on June 13, 1985. Following the guidance of the code, the dean referred the case to the school's faculty Committee on Admissions and Standards.

On June 19, 1985, the faculty committee held a day-long meeting to consider the appeal. It reviewed a copy of the materials previously presented and listened to the audio tape of the June 12 hearing before the student board. Nash and Perry were present at this meeting, and presented oral and written statements and answered questions from the faculty committee. After deliberations, the faculty committee voted unanimously to recommend that the dean uphold the board's findings and recommendations. The dean upheld the board's action. Nash and Perry then appealed to the president of Auburn University, who reviewed the written file in the case and upheld the previous decisions.

Legal Action in Federal District Court

Nash and Perry filed a lawsuit in the U. S. District Court for the Middle District of Alabama on September 20, 1985. They filed under 42 U.S.C. 1983, alleging that their civil rights, specifically their procedural and substantive due process rights, had been violated. They also filed a claim under state law for breach of contract by wrongful suspension. They asked for and received from the district court a temporary restraining order that allowed them to audit classes and take tests in veterinary school until the case was decided.

Nash and Perry sued the university, the dean, and other university administrators in their official and individual capacities for injunctive relief (to prevent the suspension) and for money damages. They claimed that the defendants procedurally and substantively violated their guarantee of due process under the Fourteenth Amendment to the U. S. Constitution:

1. Procedurally, they claimed that the steps taken by the board, the committee, the dean, and the president of the university that resulted in suspension were constitutionally inadequate. They also raised issues about the denial of a requested recess during the hearing before the student board and the fact that another cheating controversy was occurring at Auburn around the time of their hearing.
2. Substantively, they said the decision to suspend was made without sufficient evidence, that the decision was simply unfair.

The university asked the court for a summary judgment, suggesting that there were no facts in dispute and that Nash and Perry had no legal grounds on which they could succeed in the case. The district court judge held a hearing in October 1985 during which he heard testimony from both sides about the procedural steps that led to the suspension and about how the decision was made. At this hearing, Nash and Perry offered the testimony of a statistician, Dr. Harvey McKean, from the University of Kentucky. Dr. McKean had studied the exam papers and testified that the similarities found in the papers of Nash and Perry did not give rise to the conclusion that they cheated. Dr. McKean explained the similarity by the students' close collaboration and the fact that they studied from the same notes. Despite this testimony and the denials by the students, the university's motion was granted and summary judgment entered against Nash and Perry.

Appellate Court Action
The students appealed this ruling to the U. S. Court of Appeals for the Eleventh Circuit. That court carefully examined the facts of the case and made the following determinations with regard to procedural due process:

Timing of the notice. Nash and Perry argued that the notification they received of the charges against them was inadequate and especially that the "corrected" notice spelling out the charges against them was unfair because they were not given sufficient time to prepare their defense. The court stated that there are no hard and fast rules by which to measure meaningful notice, noting that in *Memphis Light, Gas & Water Div. v. Craft* (1978), "an elementary and fundamental requirement of due process . . . is notice reasonably calculated, under all the circumstances, to apprise interested parties of the pendency of the action and afford them an opportunity to present their objections" (p. 13). Looking at all the circumstances, especially the agreement by Nash and Perry and their attorney to receiving more specific notice and then having the hearing the following day, the court found no violation of the students' constitutional rights.

Content of the notice. Nash and Perry argued that the notice in the case was deficient because it did not advise them of the nature of the testimony to be presented against them or of the facts underlying the charge of academic dishonesty. Citing several case precedents, they argued that they were entitled to a summary of the testimony expected from Professor Buxton and other witnesses against them. The court acknowledged that such notice had been required in several previous cases but pointed out that in those cases the students were not present for the adverse testimony and were required to respond at a later date. In this case, Nash and Perry were present to hear and respond to the testimony against them. Discussing the flexibility of due process, the court stated that the standards of procedural due process are not wooden absolutes. The sufficiency of procedures employed in any particular situation must be judged in light of the parties, the subject matter, and the circumstances involved. The appeals court agreed with the conclusion of the lower court that Nash and Perry were not constitutionally entitled to advance notice of statements by witnesses who, along with Nash and Perry, were to appear at the hearing.

The right to cross-examination at the hearing. In the landmark case *Goss v. Lopez* (1975), the Supreme Court described the due process requirements involved in suspending public school students from high school. The Eleventh Circuit Court quoted from that case in its discussion of whether Nash and Perry were denied due process in the way that limitations were placed on the cross-examination of adverse witnesses. According to *Goss*, "The fundamental requisite of due process is the opportunity to be heard," but the nature of the hearing "will depend on appropriate accommodation of the competing interests involved" *(Morrissey v. Brewer,* 1972, p. 481). In other cases where citizens stood to lose important property rights, the Supreme Court found that cross-examination rights could not be denied, but the Eleventh Circuit decided that Nash and Perry had not been denied due process in this case. The court again quoted from *Goss:* "Due process requires that appellants have the right to respond, but their rights in the academic disciplinary process are not co-extensive with the rights of litigants in a civil trial or with those of defendants in a criminal trial" (p. 583). Although Nash and Perry were not allowed to ask questions of the adverse witnesses in a direct, adversarial manner, it was

clear to the Eleventh Circuit Court that they heard all of the testimony against them.

Denial of a recess during the hearing. The Eleventh Circuit agreed with the district court judge who found that although the granting of Nash and Perry's request for a recess during the hearing might have allowed them to more effectively exercise their limited cross-examination opportunity, the denial of the request did not constitute a denial of due process. The students were able to confront their accusers, albeit indirectly, and the denial of the requested recess was within the discretion of the hearing officer.

Fairness of the hearing tribunal. Nash and Perry raised several issues regarding the fairness of the student board that conducted their disciplinary hearing. They felt the board was biased in that there was a contemporaneous cheating controversy occurring at the university while their hearing took place. They felt that the board was prejudiced when it heard testimony about the conduct of Nash and Perry during examinations other than the anatomy final, and they contended that one of the student justices should have been disqualified from deliberations because he apparently had heard information about the case from other students before the hearing. In response to these arguments, the appellate court acknowledged that an impartial decision maker is an essential guarantee of due process. The court would not, however, infer that the board was biased based on speculation. There was nothing in the hearing record to indicate the contemporaneous cheating controversy influenced this case. For similar reasons the court felt that Nash and Perry's constitutional rights were not violated by the participation of the allegedly biased student justice or the testimony about their behavior during other exams.

Depth of the appellate review. Nash and Perry argued that the Auburn dean and president gave only fleeting review to the determinations of the student board and the faculty committee that considered their case, feeling that it violated their constitutional right to a meaningful appeal, and suggested that the administrators should have undertaken new or de novo hearings as to the facts. The court found that the procedures set up by the university did conform to the requirements of the "rudiments of fair play," which is all that the Constitution requires.

The combination of violations. As their final objection to the due process procedure they obtained through the Auburn University system, Nash and Perry argued that beyond any single violation that occurred, the inadequate notice they received as to the charges they faced, coupled with limitations on the method by which they could cross-examine their accusers, resulted in an unfair hearing. The court considered this argument carefully but decided that, based on the record of the proceedings, the students had been provided with the process to which they were constitutionally entitled.

The Eleventh Circuit Court of Appeals recognized that beyond the foregoing procedural due process claims, Nash and Perry had a constitutional right to substantive due process. "Not only does the due process clause of the Fourteenth Amendment provide procedural protections, it provides a guarantee against arbitrary decisions that would impair appellants' constitutionally protectable interests" (*Nash v. Auburn University,* 1987, p. 667). The court acknowledged that the power of the government, through its university system, to expel students was not unlimited but that "there must be some reasonable and constitutional ground for expulsion" (*Dixon v. Alabama State Board of Education,* 1961, p. 157). Nash and Perry insisted that the decisions by the student board, the faculty committee, the dean, and the president of the university were not based on substantial evidence and were therefore arbitrary. Examining the evidence that was adduced at the hearing, however, the court found that the testimony from faculty, students, and the professor who compared the students' answers was substantial and satisfied the demands of substantive due process.

Analysis
Although Nash and Perry were completely unsuccessful in their challenge to the procedural steps provided by Auburn University before their suspension for academic misconduct, this case illustrates the care with which the courts examine due process requirements in the field of higher education. At one point in the decision, the court evidences great sympathy for Nash and Perry, calling them "hard-working graduate students, beginning the training for their careers" (p. 667). Had the evidence against them been weaker or if their attorney had not had some success in working around the procedural limitations imposed by Auburn University, it is quite conceivable that the result in this case might have been different.

The Eleventh Circuit Court of Appeals, like most courts that have considered such cases, deferred to the judgment of the university, but the court specifically held that the students did have protected liberty and property interests in continued enrollment in this public school. Before ruling against the students, the court individually examined the objectivity of the decision making tribunals, the adequacy of the notice of charges, the fairness of the hearing, and the nature of the appellate process set up by the university's policies.

REFERENCES

The Educational Resources Information Center (ERIC) Clearing-house on Higher Education abstracts and indexes the current literature on higher education for inclusion in ERIC's database and announcement in ERIC's monthly bibliographic journal, *Resources in Education* (RIE). Most of these publications are available through the ERIC Document Reproduction Service (EDRS). For publications cited in this bibliography that are available from EDRS, ordering number and price code are included. Readers who wish to order a publication should write to the ERIC Document Reproduction Service, 7420 Fullerton Road, Suite 110, Springfield, Virginia 22153-2852. (Phone orders with VISA or MasterCard are taken at (800) 443-ERIC or (703) 440-1400.) When ordering, please specify the document (ED) number. Documents are available as noted in microfiche (MF) and paper copy (PC). If you have the price code ready when you call, EDRS can quote an exact price. The last page of the latest issue of *Resources in Education* also has the current cost, listed by code.

Court Cases

Bernard v. Inhabitants of Shelburne, 216 Mass. 19, 102 N.E. 1095 (1913).

Board of Curators of the University of Missouri v. Horowitz, 435 U.S. 78 (1978).

Board of Regents of State Colleges v. Roth, 408 U.S. 564 (1972).

Connelly v. University of Vermont, 244 F. Supp. 156 (D.Vt. 1995).

Davis v. Monroe County Board of Education, ___ U.S. ___ (May 24, 1999).

Dixon v. Alabama State Board of Education, 294 F.2d 150 (5th Cir. 1961).

Goldberg v. Kelly, 397 U.S. 254 (1970).

Goss v. Lopez, 419 U.S. 565 (1975).

Greenhill v. Bailey, 519 F.2d 5 (8th Cir. 1975).

In re Gault, 387 U.S. 1 (1967).

Joint Anti-Fascist Refugee Committee v. McGrath, 341 U.S. 123 (1951).

Mathews v. Eldridge, 424 U.S. 319 (1976).

Memphis Light, Gas & Water Div. v. Craft, 436 U.S. 1 (1978).

Miranda v. Arizona, 384 U.S. 436 (1966).

Morrissey v. Brewer, 408 U.S. 471 (1972).

Nash v. Auburn University, 812 F.2d 655 (11th Cir. 1987).

Perry v. Sindermann, 408 U.S. 593 (1972).

Regents of the University of Michigan v. Ewing, 474 U.S. 214 (1985).

Ross v. Pennsylvania State University, 445 F. Supp 147 (M.D. Pa. 1978).

Susan "M" v. New York Law School, 556 N.E.2d 1104 (N.Y. 1990).

U. S. v. Wade, 388 U.S. 218 (1967).

Wood v. Strickland, 420 U.S. 308 (1975).

Books and Journals

Abramson, L. Y., Seligman, M. E. P., & Teasdale, J. (1978). Learned helplessness in humans: Critique and reformulation. *Journal of Abnormal Psychology, 87,* 49-74.

Allen, B. T. (1995). *Preventing sexual harassment on campus: Policies and practices for higher education.* Washington, DC: College and University Personnel Association. ED 388 159. 67 pp. MF–01; PC not available EDRS.

American Association of University Professors. (1989). *Statement on plagiarism.* Washington, DC: Author.

Association of American Medical Colleges. (1993). *Americans with Disabilities Act: The disabled student in medical school. Guidelines for medical schools.* Washington, DC: Author. ED 370 491. 23 pp. MF–01; PC–01.

Association of American Medical Colleges, Executive Council. (1992, September 24). *Beyond the framework: Institutional considerations in managing allegations of misconduct in research.* Washington, DC: Author.

Association of American Universities. (1989, November 10). *Framework for institutional policies and procedures to deal with fraud in research.* Washington, DC: Author.

Baez, B., & Centra, J. A. (1995). *Tenure, promotion, and reappointment: Legal and administrative implications.* ASHE-ERIC Higher Education Report (vol. 24, no. 1). Washington, DC: The George Washington University, Graduate School of Education and Human Development. ED 396 608. 214 pp. MF–01; PC–09.

Bailyn, B. (1967). *The ideological origins of the American Revolution.* Cambridge, MA: Harvard University Press.

Baker, T. R. (1992). The meaning of due process 30 years after *Dixon:* Rhetoric but little research. *NASPA Journal, 30*(1), 3-10.

Barnum, R., & Grisso, T. (1996). Competence to stand trial in juvenile court in Massachusetts: Issues of therapeutic jurisprudence. In D. B. Wexler & B. J. Winick (Eds.), *Law in a therapeutic key: Developments in therapeutic jurisprudence* (pp. 113-130). Durham, NC: Carolina Academic Press.

Barr, M. J. (Ed.). (1988). *Student services and the law: A handbook for practitioners.* San Francisco: Jossey-Bass.

Bazluke, F. T. (1990). *Defamation issues in higher education.* Washington, DC: National Association of College and University Attorneys. ED 410 849. 24 pp. MF–01; PC not available EDRS.

Berger, R. (1977). *Government by judiciary*. Cambridge, MA: Harvard University Press.

Bienstock, R. E. (1996). *A guide to conducting a hearing in a higher education setting*. Asheville, NC: College Administration Publications.

Brandenburg, J. B. (1995). *Sexual harassment: A challenge to schools of education*. Washington, DC: American Association of Colleges for Teacher Education. ED 380 439. 32 pp. MF–01; PC–02.

Brooks, B. G. (1995). Adequate cause for dismissal: The missing element in academic freedom. *Journal of College and University Law, 22*(2), 331-358.

Brown, V. L., & Buttolph, K. (Eds.). (1993). *Student disciplinary issues: A legal compendium*. Washington, DC: National Association of College and University Attorneys. ED 363 186. 474 pp. MF–01; PC not available EDRS.

Carpenter, L. J., & Acosta, R. V. (1993). Playing by the rules: Equity in sports. *CUPA Journal, 44*(2), 55-60.

Coke, E. (1671). *Second part of the institutes of the laws of England*. (4th ed.). London.

Cole, E. K. (Ed.). (1990). *Sexual harassment on campus: A legal compendium*. (2nd Ed.). Washington, DC: National Association of College and University Attorneys.

Cole, E. K. (1994). *Selected legal issues relating to due process and liability in higher education*. Washington, DC: Council of Graduate Schools.

Cole, E. K., & Shields, B. L. (Eds.). (1989). *Student legal issues*. Washington, DC: National Association of College and University Attorneys.

Congress of the United States. (1993). *A compilation of federal education laws: Vol. 1, General provisions, as amended through December 31, 1992*. Washington, DC: U. S. Government Printing Office. ED 357 028. 187 pp. MF–01; PC–08.

Corwin, E. S. (1948). *Liberty against government: The rise, flowering, and decline of a famous judicial concept*. Baton Rouge, LA: Louisiana State University Press.

Danelski, D. J. (1977). Due process in a nonlegal setting: An ombudsman's experience. In J. R. Pennock & J. W. Chapman (Eds.), *Due process* (pp. 257-263). New York: New York University Press.

Davis, K. C. (1969). *Discretionary justice: A preliminary inquiry*. Baton Rouge, LA: Louisiana State University Press.

Drapeau, D. A. (1995, January). Tenure traps: Legal issues of concern. *Journal of the Association for Communication Administration, 1,* 60-63.

Dunham, W. H., Jr. (1965). *The great charter.* New York: Pantheon Books.

Eames, P., & Hustoles, T. P. (Eds.). (1989). *Legal issues in faculty employment.* Washington, DC: National Association of College and University Attorneys.

Ford, D. L., & Strope, J. L. (1996, August 22). Judicial responses to adverse academic decisions affecting public postsecondary institution students since *Horowitz* and *Ewing. West's Education Law Reporter, 110,* 517-542.

Gellhorn, E., & Boyer, B. B. (1981). *Administrative law and process in a nutshell.* St. Paul, MN: West Publishing Company.

Golden, E. J. (1982). Procedural due process for students at public colleges and universities. *Journal of Law and Education, 11*(3), 337-359.

Gould, K. A. (1996). Turning rat and doing time for uncharged, dismissed, or acquitted crimes: Do the federal sentencing guidelines promote respect for the law? In D. B. Wexler & B. J. Winick (Eds.), *Law in a therapeutic key: Developments in therapeutic jurisprudence* (pp. 171-201). Durham, NC: Carolina Academic Press.

Grant, C. M. (1995). Predismissal hearings for school employees: Developments since *Loudermill. School Law Bulletin, 26*(3), 1-9.

Grey, T. C. (1977). Procedural fairness and substantive rights. In J. R. Pennock & J. W. Chapman (Eds.), *Due process* (pp. 182-205). New York: New York University Press.

Guthrie-Morse, B. (1996). Handling the confidential student complaint of faculty sexual harassment: An administrative course of action. *Initiatives, 57*(2), 49-54.

Hagen, J. W., & Hagen, W. W., III. (1995, March). What employment counselors need to know about employment discrimination and the Civil Rights Act of 1992. *Journal of Employment Counseling, 32*(1), 2-10.

Haines, C. G. (1930). *The revival of natural law concepts.* Cambridge, MA: Harvard University Press.

Hendrickson, R. M. (1988, April 14). Removing tenured faculty for cause. *West's Education Law Reporter, 44*(2), 483-494.

Hollander, P. A., Young, D. P., & Gehring, D. D. (1995). *A practical guide to legal issues affecting college teachers.* Asheville, NC: College Administration Publications.

Holub, J. (1996, June). *Addressing sexual harassment on campus.* Los Angeles: ERIC Clearinghouse for Community Colleges. ED 400 002. 4 pp. MF–01; PC–01.

Horner, S. S. (1993). Nonrenewal of part-time faculty. *Business Officer, 26*(12): 36-38.

Howard, A. E. D. (1968). *The road from Runnymede: Magna Carta and constitutionalism in America.* Charlottesville, VA: University Press of Virginia.

Hustoles, T. P. (1992). *Introduction to tenure, due process, just cause, developing tort and contract theories, privacy rights, faculty evaluation, and collective bargaining.* Paper presented at the Second Annual Conference on Legal Issues in Higher Education, Burlington, VT.

Hustoles, T. P., & Connolly, W. B., Jr. (Eds.). (1990). *Regulating racial harassment on campus.* Washington, DC: National Association of College and University Attorneys. ED 328 204. 314 pp. MF–01; PC not available EDRS.

Hustoles, T. P., & Duerr, C. A., Jr. (1994). Dealing with employee misconduct on and off duty: A practical framework. *CUPA Journal, 45*(4), 1-10.

Irby, D. M., & Milam, S. (1989). The legal context for evaluating and dismissing medical students and residents. *Academic Medicine, 64*(11), 639-643.

Kaplin, W. (1978). *The law of higher education.* San Francisco: Jossey-Bass.

Kaplin, W. A. (1985). *The law of higher education: A comprehensive guide to legal implications of administrative decision making* (2nd ed.). San Francisco: Jossey-Bass.

Kaplin, W. A., & Lee, B. A. (1991). *The law of higher education: 1986-1990 update.* Washington, DC: National Association of College and University Attorneys.

Katz, K. D. (1983, Summer). The First Amendment's protection of expressive activity in the classroom: A constitutional myth. *U. C. Davis Law Review, 16*(4), 2-7.

Kaufman, H. E. (1991). *Access to institutions of higher education for students with disabilities.* Washington, DC: National Association of College and University Attorneys. ED 377 630. 33 pp. MF–01; PC not available EDRS.

Keyes, G. (1989). Procedural due process in the dismissal of residents. *Journal of Dental Education, 53*(3), 178-181.

Kibler, W. L. (1988). *Academic integrity and student development: Legal issues and policy perspectives.* Higher Education Administration Series. Asheville, NC: College Administration Publications.

Kirp, D. L. (1976). Proceduralism and bureaucracy: Due process in the school setting. *Stanford Law Review, 26,* 841-876.

Klein, I. J. (1989). *Law of evidence for criminal justice professionals*

(3rd ed.). St. Paul, MN: West Publishing Company.

Klotter, J. C., & Kanovitz, J. R. (1995). *Constitutional law* (7th ed.). Cincinnati, OH: W. H. Anderson Publishing Company.

Lallo, D. (1992). Student challenges to grades and academic dismissals: Are they losing battles? *Journal of College and University Law, 18,* 577-593.

Lamont, L. (1979). *Campus shock.* New York: Dutton.

Latourette, A. W., & King, R. (1988). Judicial intervention in the student-university relationship: Due process and contract theories. *University of Detroit Law Review, 65,* 199-258.

Leap, T. L. (1995). *Tenure, discrimination, and the courts* (2nd ed.). Ithaca, NY: Cornell University Press, ILR Press.

Lee, B. A. (1990). *Peer review confidentiality: Is it possible?* Washington, DC: National Association of College and University Attorneys. ED 341 336. 25 pp. MF–01; PC not available EDRS.

Lewis, J. F., & Hastings, S. C. (1994). *Sexual harassment in education* (2nd ed.). Cleveland, OH: Squires, Sanders & Dempsey.

Lind, E. A. (1990). In the eye of the beholder: Tort litigants' evaluations of their courtroom experiences in the civil justice system. *Law & Society Review, 24,* 968-971.

Lind, E. A., Maccoun, R. J., Ebener, P. A., Felstiner, W., Hensler, D., Resnik, J., & Tyler, T. (1990). In the eye of the beholder: Tort litigants' evaluations of their courtroom experiences in the civil justice system. *Law and Society Review, 24,* 953-996.

Lind, E. A., & Tyler, T. R. (1988). *The social psychology of procedural justice.* New York: Plenum Publishing.

Ludeman, R. B. (1989). The formal academic grievance process in higher education: A survey of current practices. *NASPA Journal, 26*(3), 235-240.

Maier, S. F., & Seligman, M. E. P. (1976). Learned helplessness: Theory and evidence. *Journal of Experimental Psychology, 105,* 33-46.

Marshall, G. (1977). Due process in England. In J. R. Pennock & J. W. Chapman (Eds.), *Due process* (pp. 69-92). New York: New York University Press.

McIntyre, J. S. (1993). *University policies and procedures on sexual harassment.* ED 371 696. 14 pp. MF–01; PC–01.

Michaelson, M. (1991, December 5). Observations on the handling of research misconduct cases. *The NACUA College Law Digest and West's Education Law Report.*

Michelman, F. I. (1977). Formal and associational aims in procedural due process. In J. R. Pennock & J. W. Chapman (Eds.), *Due process* (pp. 126-171). New York: New York University Press.

Miller, C. A. (1977). The forest of due process of law: The American constitutional tradition. In J. R. Pennock & J. W. Chapman (Eds.), *Due process* (pp. 3-67). New York: New York University Press.

Mullany, J. W., & Timberlake, E. M. (1994). University tenure and the legal system: Procedures, conflicts, and resolutions. *Journal of Social Work Education, 30*(2), 172-184.

Murray, C. (1994). Campus justice: West Virginia Wesleyan case questions fairness of judiciary boards. *Black Issues in Higher Education, 11*(9), 6-9.

National Academy of Sciences, National Academy of Engineering, & Institute of Medicine. (1993). *Responsible science: Ensuring the integrity of the research process* (Vol. 2). Washington, DC: National Academy Press.

Newman, S. A. (1995). At work in the marketplace of ideas: Academic freedom, the First Amendment, and *Jeffries v. Harleston. Journal of College and University Law, 22*(2), 281-359.

Nordin, V. D. (1980). The contract to educate: Toward a more workable theory of the student-university relationship. *Journal of College and University Law, 8,* 141-181.

O'Neil, R. M. (1983a). Academic freedom and the Constitution. *Journal of College and University Law, 3,* 275-292.

O'Neil, R. M. (1983b). Scientific research and the First Amendment: An academic privilege. *U. C. Davis Law Review, 16*(94), 837-855.

Packer, H. L. (1968). *The limits of the criminal sanction.* Stanford, CA: Stanford University Press.

Paretsky, J. M. (1993, October). Judicial review of discretionary grants of higher education tenure. *West's Education Law Quarterly, 2*(4), 621-630.

Pavela, G. (1980). Limiting the pursuit of perfect justice on campus. *Journal of College and University Law, 6,* 137-160.

Pavela, G. (1985). *The dismissal of students with mental disorders: Legal issues, policy considerations, and alternative responses.* Asheville, NC: College Administration Publications.

Pavela, G. (1990). *The dismissal of students with mental disorders.* Washington, DC: National Association of College and University Attorneys. ED 410 848. 31 pp. MF–01; PC not available EDRS.

Pennock, J. R., & Chapman, J. W. (Eds.). (1977). *Due process.* New York: New York University Press.

Perelman, C. (1967). *Justice.* New York: Random House.

Perry, R. L. (1964). *Sources of our liberties.* New York: McGraw-Hill.

Picozzi, J. M. (1987). Note—University disciplinary process: What's fair, what's due, and what you don't get. *Yale Law Journal, 96,* 2132-2161.

Poch, R. K. (1993). *Academic freedom in America higher education: Rights, responsibilities, and limitations.* ASHE-ERIC Higher Education Report (vol. 22, no. 4). Washington, DC: The George Washington University, Graduate School of Education and Human Development. ED 366 263. 109 pp. MF–01; PC–05.

Pollack, L. H. (1957). Mr. Justice Frankfurter: Judgment in the Fourteenth Amendment. *Yale Law Journal, 67,* 304-343.

Pressman, R. (1990). *State law challenges to school discipline: An outline of claims and case summaries.* Cambridge, MA: Harvard University, Center for Law and Education. ED 333 590. 38 pp. MF–01; PC–02.

Price, S. S., & Andes, J. O. (1990). An update on academic dismissal for clinical reasons. *Journal of Dental Education, 54,* 747-749.

Radin, M. (1947). The myth of Magna Carta. *Harvard Law Review, 60,* 1069-1091.

Rawls, J. (1971). *A theory of justice.* Cambridge, MA: Harvard University Press.

Riggs, R. O., Murrell, P. H., & Cutting, J. C. (1993). *Sexual harassment in higher education: From conflict to community.* ASHE-ERIC Higher Education Report (vol. 22, no. 2). Washington, DC: The George Washington University, Graduate School of Education and Human Development. ED 364 133. 114 pp. MF–01; PC–05.

Rigney, D. B., & Butner, B. B. (1993). *Federal student aid programs.* Washington, DC: National Association of College and University Attorneys.

Rosenbloom, D. H., & Carroll, J. D. (1990). *Toward constitutional competence: A casebook for public administrators.* Englewood Cliffs, NJ: Prentice-Hall.

Roth, S. H. (1994). Sex Discrimination 101: Developing a Title IX analysis for sexual harassment in education. *Journal of Law and Education, 23,* 459-521.

Rothstein, L. (1991). Commentary: Students, staff, and faculty with disabilities. *Journal of College and University Law, 17,* 471-482.

Rubin, D., & Greenhouse, S. (1983). *The rights of teachers: The basic ACLU guide to a teacher's constitutional rights.* New York: Bantam Books.

Ruiz, C. M. (1995). *Legal standards regarding gender equity and affirmative action.* ED 381 864. 14 pp. MF–01; PC–01.

Sagan, J. S., & Rebel, T. P. (Eds.). (1995). *Employment issues in higher education: A legal compendium.* Washington, DC: National Association of College and University Attorneys. ED 378 932. 532 pp. MF–02; PC not available EDRS.

Saurack, W. (1995). Protecting the student: A critique of the procedural protection afforded to American and English students in university disciplinary hearings. *Journal of College and University Law, 21,* 785-824.

Scanlon, T. M. (1977). Due process. In J. R. Pennock & J. W. Chapman (Eds.), *Due process* (pp. 93-125). New York: New York University Press.

Schimmel, D. (1994). Sexual harassment in the workplace: When are hostile comments actionable? *West's Education Law Quarterly, 3,* 431-439.

Schwartz, B. (1991). *Administrative law* (3rd ed.). Boston: Little, Brown & Co.

Schweitzer, T. A. (1992). "Academic challenge" cases: Should judicial review extend to academic evaluations of students? *American University Law Review, 41,* 267-367.

Seligman, M. E. P., & Garber, J. (Eds.). (1980). *Human helplessness: Theory and applications.* New York: Academic Press.

Shea, C. (1994, October 19). A matter of honor. *Chronicle of Higher Education, 41*(8), 55-56.

Simon, W. (1978). The ideology of advocacy: Procedural justice and professional ethics. *Wisconsin Law Review, 29,* 29-144.

Steele, B. H., Johnson, H. D., & Richard, S. T. (1984, July). Managing the judicial function in student affairs. *Journal of College Student Personnel, 25,* 337-342.

Stoner, E. N., & Cerminara, K. L. (1990). Harnessing the "spirit of insubordination": Model student disciplinary code. *Journal of College and University Law, 17,* 89-121.

Strohm, L. C. (Ed.). (1991). *AIDS on campus: A legal compendium.* Washington, DC: National Association of College and University Attorneys. ED 377 427. 484 pp. MF–02; PC not available EDRS.

Svenson, E. V. (1995). Student v. instructor: Higher education law in the trenches. *Teaching Psychology, 22*(3), 169-172.

Taylor, M. C. (1995). Sexual harassment and institutional liability: A review of federal court opinions and implications for HBCUs. *Western Journal of Black Studies, 19*(3), 164-171.

Thibaut, J., & Walker, L. (1975). *Procedural justice: A psychological analysis.* Hillsdale, NJ: Erlbaum.

Toenjes, R. H. (1990). *The UNC–Charlotte code of student academic integrity.* Washington, DC: American Association of State Colleges and Universities. ED 321 655. 35 pp. MF–01; PC–02.

Tribe, L. (1973). Toward a model of roles in the due process of life and law. *Harvard Law Review, 87,* 1-53.

Tyler, T. R. (1996). The psychological consequences of judicial procedures: Implications for civil commitment hearings. In D. B. Wexler & B. J. Winick (Eds.), *Law in a therapeutic key: Developments in therapeutic jurisprudence* (pp. 3-15). Durham, NC: Carolina Academic Press.

Tyler, T. R., & Lind, E. A. (1992). A rational model of authority in groups. *Advances in Experimental Social Psychology, 115,* 137-166.

Van Alstyne, W. (1968). The student as university resident. *Denver Law Journal, 45,* 582-638.

Van Alstyne, W. (1972). The specific theory of academic freedom and the general issue of civil liberty. In E. L. Pincoffs (Ed.), *The concept of academic freedom.* Austin, TX: University of Texas Press.

Van Tol, J. E. (Ed.). (1989). *College and university student records: A legal compendium.* Washington, DC: National Association of College and University Attorneys.

Wesson, M., & Johnson, S. (1991, May/June). Post tenure review and faculty revitalization. *Academe, 77*(3), 53-57.

Wexler, D. B., & Winick, B. J. (1991). Therapeutic jurisprudence as a new approach to mental health law policy analysis and research. *University of Miami Law Review, 45,* 979-1004.

Wexler, D. B., & Winick, B. J. (Eds.). (1996). *Law in a therapeutic key: Developments in therapeutic jurisprudence.* Durham, NC: Carolina Academic Press.

Whicker, M. L., & Kronenfeld, J. J. (1994). *Survival skills for scholars: Vol. 14. Dealing with ethical dilemmas on campus.* Thousand Oaks, CA: Sage.

Williams, V. L. (1999, June 18). A new harassment ruling: Implications for colleges. *Chronicle of Higher Education, 45,* A56.

Winick, B. J. (1996). The jurisprudence of therapeutic jurisprudence. In D. B. Wexler & B. J. Winick (Eds.), *Law in a therapeutic key: Developments in therapeutic jurisprudence* (pp. 645-668). Durham, NC: Carolina Academic Press.

Wolfe, C. (1991). The original meaning of the Due Process Clause. In E. W. Hickok, Jr. (Ed.), *The Bill of Rights: Original meaning and current understanding* (pp. 213-230). Charlottesville, VA, & London: University Press of Virginia.

Wright, C. A. (1969). The Constitution on the campus. *Vanderbilt Law Review, 22,* 1027-1088.

Yudof, M. G. (1987). Three faces of academic freedom. *Loyola Law Review, 32,* 831-851.

Zalman, M., & Siegel, L. (1997). *Criminal procedure: Constitution and society* (2nd ed.). St. Paul, MN: West Publishing Company.

INDEX

capricious. *See* arbitrary and capricious.

civil liberties, 14

civil litigation, 2, 63, 65, 115

clear and convincing standard, 65-66,71

"clearly erroneous," 39, 71

closed hearing, 49

codes of conduct, 17, 24-26, 29, 42, 77. *See also Dixon v. Alabama State Board of Education.*

compulsory process, right to, 52

constitutional

    law, 4, 7, 17-18, 24, 30, 32, 33, 64, 70, 73, 78, 93

    rights, 1, 7, 10, 14, 16, 20-21, 23, 25, 28, 30-33, 35, 61, 63-64. *See also Dixon v. Alabama State Board of Education* and *Nash v. Auburn University.*

contract law, 1, 7, 24, 29, 73

contractual requirements, 3-4, 18, 20, 23

cross-examination, right to, 21, 22, 26, 61-63, 78, 83, 114-115

D

Davis v. Monroe County Board of Education, 84, 103, 110. *See also* harassment, student-on-student.

disciplinary sanctions, 27-30

discovery, right to, 50-51

discretionary decisions, 5, 30, 35, 60

discrimination

    disability, 2, 4, 9, 32, 79

    mental disability, 12, 50, 73

dismissal, 9, 29, 44

Dixon v. Alabama State Board of Education, 10, 25-26, 29, 42, 116

documentary evidence, 51

double jeopardy, 64

due process

    Clause of Fifth Amendment, 13

    Clause of Fourteenth Amendment, 1, 14-16, 20, 23, 116

    depth of procedural protection, 16, 18, 21-23, 27-29, 97, 102

    procedural, 1, 5-6, 9-10, 15, 16, 18-19, 21, 23-24, 29, 31, 34, 35, 38-40, 43-45, 67, 75, 112-116

    right to, 14, 21

    substantive, 1, 5, 13, 15-16, 17-18, 19, 23-24, 28, 31, 34, 35, 38-40, 42-43, 67, 112, 116

E

entitlements, 20

ethical standards, 34, 68
evidence
     and ethical questions, 52
     exculpatory, right to, 51-52
     right to present, 39, 58, 75
     rules of, 25, 45, 57-58, 62
expulsion, 25, 29, 42, 44-45, 47, 66, 83, 116

F

fact finder, function of, 56
fair hearing, 1, 6, 31, 50, 57
fair trial, right to, 61
Family Educational Rights and Privacy Act of 1974, 49
Federal Rules of Evidence, 57
Fifth Amendment, 13, 33, 63
First Amendment, 31, 32
Fourteenth Amendment, 1, 2-3, 14-16, 23, 33, 113, 116
freedom of speech, right to, 31, 110

G

Goldberg v. Kelly, 15, 22, 75
good faith effort, 35
Goss v. Lopez, 11, 29, 43-44, 114-115

H

harassment, 78
     sexual, 2, 4, 9-10, 79, 82
     student-on-student, 78, 84, 86, 102-103, 106, 110
hearing,
     decision, 19, 39-41, 66, 67-71
     denial of recess, 112-113, 115
     formal, 28, 44, 45-46
     format, 18, 43, 56-59, 72, 92
     informal, 5, 44, 46-47
     limiting scope of, 46, 57-58
     open, right to, 48-50
     panel, 37-41, 44, 47-48, 64, 66
     postponement, right to, 54
     right to, 10, 85
     right to record, 19, 54-56
     role of administrator. *See* administrator, role of in hearing.
     safeguards, 37, 44. *See also* due process, depth of
        procedural protection.

preliminary investigation, 52

preponderance of evidence standard, 39, 65-66, 71

present evidence, right to, 39, 58, 75

privacy, right to, 15

probable cause, 65

procedural

       complexity, 5, 38, 41, 44-47

       due process, right to, 67, 110

       formality. *See* hearing, formal.

       protection. *See* due process, depth of procedural protection.

       safeguards. *See* due process, depth of procedural protection.

proof, standards of, 65-66

property interests, 1, 3, 13-16, 19-22, 34, 45, 48, 63, 75, 86, 116

protected speech, 20

R

reasonableness standard, 32, 35

record hearings, right to, 19, 54-56

refuse to participate, right to, 63-64

Regents of the University of Michigan v. Ewing, 11, 28

remain silent, right to, 61, 63-64

representation, right to, 59-61

right to,

       an attorney, 19, 22, 26, 59-61, 78

       appeal, 68-70, 112, 115

       compulsory process, 52

       cross-examination, 21, 22, 26, 61-63, 78, 83, 114-115

       discovery, 50-51

       exculpatory evidence, 51-52

       independent investigation, 52-54

       jury trial, 15

       open hearing, 48-50

       postponement, 54

       present evidence, 39, 58, 75

       procedural due process, 67, 110

       record hearings, 19, 54-56

       refuse to participate, 63-64

       remain silent, 61, 63-64

       representation, 59-61

       subpoena, 26

       substantive due process, 110, 116

       sworn testimony, 63

       transcript, 70

Ross v. Pennsylvania State University, 21, 24
rules of evidence, 25, 45, 57-58, 62

S

sanctions, extent of, 27-30, 42, 55, 70
self-incrimination, 39, 63-64
sexual harassment. *See* harassment, sexual.
Sixth Amendment, 15, 61
standards of proof, 65-66
student-on-student harassment. *See* harassment, student-on-student.
subpoena, right to, 26
substantial evidence, 39, 65, 116
substantive due process, right to, 110, 116
substantive fairness, 39, 43, 53, 69, 70
suspensions for misconduct, 29, 44, 111-116
sworn testimony, right to, 63

T

tenure, 2, 3, 9-10, 12, 18, 20-21, 37, 42, 47, 50
termination, 21, 37, 47
therapeutic jurisprudence, 6, 73-75
transcript, right to, 70

U

United States v. Wade, 61
unreasonable government action, 13

V

video recordings of hearing, 54-56, 69

W

witnesses, right to call, 29
Wood v. Strickland, 11, 32
written hearing decision, right to, 19

ASHE-ERIC HIGHER EDUCATION REPORTS

Since 1983, the Association for the Study of Higher Education (ASHE) and the Educational Resources Information Center (ERIC) Clearinghouse on Higher Education, a sponsored project of the Graduate School of Education and Human Development at The George Washington University, have cosponsored the ASHE-ERIC Higher Education Report series. This volume is the twenty-seventh overall and the tenth to be published by the Graduate School of Education and Human Development at The George Washington University.

Each monograph is the definitive analysis of a tough higher education problem, based on thorough research of pertinent literature and institutional experiences. Topics are identified by a national survey. Noted practitioners and scholars are then commissioned to write the reports, with experts providing critical reviews of each manuscript before publication.

Eight monographs (10 before 1985) in the ASHE-ERIC Higher Education Report series are published each year and are available on individual and subscription bases. To order, use the order form on the last page of this book.

Qualified persons interested in writing a monograph for the ASHE-ERIC Higher Education Report series are invited to submit a proposal to the National Advisory Board. As the preeminent literature review and issue analysis series in higher education, the Higher Education Reports are guaranteed wide dissemination and national exposure for accepted candidates. Execution of a monograph requires at least a minimal familiarity with the ERIC database, including *Resources in Education* and the current *Index to Journals in Education*. The objective of these reports is to bridge conventional wisdom with practical research. Prospective authors are strongly encouraged to call at (800) 773-3742.

For further information, write to
    ASHE-ERIC Higher Education Report Series
    The George Washington University
    One Dupont Circle, Suite 630
    Washington, DC 20036-1183
Or phone (202) 296-2597
Toll free: (800) 773-ERIC

Write or call for a complete catalog.

Visit our Web site at **www.eriche.org/reports**

ADVISORY BOARD

James Earl Davis
University of Delaware at Newark

Kenneth A. Feldman
State University of New York–Stony Brook

Kassie Freeman
Peabody College, Vanderbilt University

Susan Frost
Emory University

Esther E. Gottlieb
West Virginia University

Philo Hutcheson
Georgia State University

Lori White
Stanford University

Ivan B. Liss
Radford University

Anne Goodsell Love
University of Akron

Clara M. Lovett
Northern Arizona University

Meredith Ludwig
Education Statistics Services Institute

Jean MacGregor
Evergreen State College

Laurence R. Marcus
Rowan College

William McKeachie
University of Michigan

Mantha V. Mehallis
Florida Atlantic University

Robert Menges
Northwestern University

Diane E. Morrison
Centre for Curriculum, Transfer, and Technology

Barbara M. Moskal
Colorado School of Mines

John A. Muffo
Virginia Polytechnic Institute and State University

Patricia H. Murrell
University of Memphis

L. Jackson Newell
Deep Springs College

Steven G. Olswang
University of Washington

R. Eugene Rice
American Association for Higher Education

Maria Scatena
St. Mary of the Woods College

John Schuh
Iowa State University

Jack H. Schuster
Claremont Graduate School–Center for Educational Studies

Carole Schwinn
Jackson Community College

Patricia Somers
University of Arkansas at Little Rock

Leonard Springer
University of Wisconsin–Madison

Richard J. Stiggins
Assessment and Training Institute

Marilla D. Svinicki
University of Texas–Austin

David Sweet
OERI, U.S. Department of Education

Catherine S. Taylor
University of Washington

Dan W. Wheeler
University of Nebraska–Lincoln

Christine K. Wilkinson
Arizona State University

Donald H. Wulff
University of Washington

Manta Yorke
Liverpool John Moores University

William Zeller
University of Michigan at Ann Arbor

REVIEW PANEL

Richard Alfred
University of Michigan

Thomas A. Angelo
DePaul University

Charles Bantz
Arizona State University

Robert J. Barak
Iowa State Board of Regents

Alan Bayer
Virginia Polytechnic Institute and State University

John P. Bean
Indiana University–Bloomington

John M. Braxton
Peabody College, Vanderbilt University

Ellen M. Brier
Tennessee State University

Dennis Brown
University of Kansas

Deborah Faye Carter
Indiana University

Patricia Carter
University of Michigan

John A. Centra
Syracuse University

Paul B. Chewning
Council for the Advancement and Support of Education

Arthur W. Chickering
Vermont College

Darrel A. Clowes
Virginia Polytechnic Institute and State University

Carol L. Colbeck
Pennsylvania State University

Deborah M. DiCroce
Tidewater Virginia Community College

Marty Finkelstein
Seton Hall University

Dorothy E. Finnegan
The College of William & Mary

Timothy Gallineau
Buffalo State College

Judith Glazer-Raymo
Long Island University

Kenneth C. Green
Claremont Graduate University

James C. Hearn
University of Minnesota

Donald E. Heller
University of Michigan

Edward R. Hines
Illinois State University

Deborah Hirsch
University of Massachusetts

Deborah Hunter
University of Vermont

Linda K. Johnsrud
University of Hawaii at Manoa

Bruce Anthony Jones
University of Missouri–Columbia

Elizabeth A. Jones
West Virginia University

Marsha V. Krotseng
Cleveland State University

George D. Kuh
Indiana University–Bloomington

J. Roderick Lauver
Planned Systems International, Inc.–Maryland

Daniel T. Layzell
MGT of America, Inc., Madison, Wisconsin

Ronald Lee
University of Nebraska

Patrick G. Love
Kent State University

Mantha V. Mehallis
Florida Atlantic University

Marcia Mentkowski
Alverno College

John Milam, Jr.
George Mason University

Toby Milton
Essex Community College

Christopher C. Morphew
University of Kansas

John A. Muffo
Virginia Polytechnic Institute and State University

L. Jackson Newell
Deep Springs College

Mark Oromaner
Hudson County Community College

Suzanne Ortega
University of Nebraska

James C. Palmer
Illinois State University

Michael Paulsen
University of New Orleans

Robert A. Rhoads
Michigan State University

G. Jeremiah Ryan
Quincy College

Mary Ann Danowitz Sagaria
The Ohio State University

Kathleen M. Shaw
Temple University

Edward St. John
Indiana University

Scott Swail
College Bound

J. Douglas Toma
University of Missouri–Kansas City

Kathryn Nemeth Tuttle
University of Kansas

David S. Webster
Oklahoma State University

Lisa Wolf
University of Kansas

Volume 27 ASHE-ERIC Higher Education Reports

1. The Art and Science of Classroom Assessment: The Missing Part of Pedagogy
   Susan M. Brookhart

Volume 26 ASHE-ERIC Higher Education Reports

1. Faculty Workload Studies: Perspectives, Needs, and Future Directions
   Katrina A. Meyer

2. Assessing Faculty Publication Productivity: Issues of Equity
   Elizabeth G. Creamer

3. Proclaiming and Sustaining Excellence: Assessment as a Faculty Role
   Karen Maitland Schilling and Karl L. Schilling

4. Creating Learning Centered Classrooms: What Does Learning Theory Have to Say?
   Frances K. Stage, Patricia A. Muller, Jillian Kinzie, and Ada Simmons

5. The Academic Administrator and the Law: What Every Dean and Department Chair Needs to Know
   J. Douglas Toma and Richard L. Palm

6. The Powerful Potential of Learning Communities: Improving Education for the Future
   Oscar T. Lenning and Larry H. Ebbers

7. Enrollment Management for the 21st Century: Institutional Goals, Accountability, and Fiscal Responsibility
   Garlene Penn

8. Enacting Diverse Learning Environments: Improving the Climate for Racial/Ethnic Diversity in Higher Education
   Sylvia Hurtado, Jeffrey Milem, Alma Clayton-Pedersen, and Walter Allen

Volume 25 ASHE-ERIC Higher Education Reports

1. A Culture for Academic Excellence: Implementing the Quality Principles in Higher Education
   Jann E. Freed, Marie R. Klugman, and Jonathan D. Fife

2. From Discipline to Development: Rethinking Student Conduct in Higher Education
   Michael Dannells

3. Academic Controversy: Enriching College Instruction Through Intellectual Conflict
   David W. Johnson, Roger T. Johnson, and Karl A. Smith

4. Higher Education Leadership: Analyzing the Gender Gap
   Luba Chliwniak

5. The Virtual Campus: Technology and Reform in Higher Education
   Gerald C. Van Dusen

6. Early Intervention Programs: Opening the Door to Higher Education
   Robert H. Fenske, Christine A. Geranios, Jonathan E. Keller, and David E. Moore

7. The Vitality of Senior Faculty Members: Snow on the Roof— Fire in the Furnace
   Carole J. Bland and William H. Bergquist

8. A National Review of Scholastic Achievement in General Education: How Are We Doing and Why Should We Care?
   Steven J. Osterlind

Volume 24 ASHE-ERIC Higher Education Reports

1. Tenure, Promotion, and Reappointment: Legal and Administrative Implications
   Benjamin Baez and John A. Centra

2. Taking Teaching Seriously: Meeting the Challenge of Instructional Improvement
   Michael B. Paulsen and Kenneth A. Feldman

3. Empowering the Faculty: Mentoring Redirected and Renewed
   Gaye Luna and Deborah L. Cullen

4. Enhancing Student Learning: Intellectual, Social, and Emotional Integration
   Anne Goodsell Love and Patrick G. Love

5. Benchmarking in Higher Education: Adapting Best Practices to Improve Quality
   Jeffrey W. Alstete

6. Models for Improving College Teaching: A Faculty Resource
   Jon E. Travis

7. Experiential Learning in Higher Education: Linking Classroom and Community
   Jeffrey A. Cantor

8. Successful Faculty Development and Evaluation: The Complete Teaching Portfolio
   John P. Murray

Volume 23 ASHE-ERIC Higher Education Reports

1. The Advisory Committee Advantage: Creating an Effective Strategy for Programmatic Improvement
   Lee Teitel

2. Collaborative Peer Review: The Role of Faculty in Improving College Teaching
   Larry Keig and Michael D. Waggoner

3. Prices, Productivity, and Investment: Assessing Financial Strategies in Higher Education
   Edward P. St. John

4. The Development Officer in Higher Education: Toward an Understanding of the Role
   Michael J. Worth and James W. Asp II

5. Measuring Up: The Promises and Pitfalls of Performance Indicators in Higher Education
   Gerald Gaither, Brian P. Nedwek, and John E. Neal

6. A New Alliance: Continuous Quality and Classroom Effectiveness
   Mimi Wolverton

7. Redesigning Higher Education: Producing Dramatic Gains in Student Learning
   Lion F. Gardiner

8. Student Learning Outside the Classroom: Transcending Artificial Boundaries
   George D. Kuh, Katie Branch Douglas, Jon P. Lund, and Jackie Ramin-Gyurnek

Quantity **Amount**

_____ Please begin my subscription to the current year's
ASHE-ERIC Higher Education Reports at $144.00, over
25% off the cover price, starting with Report 1. _____

_____ Please send a complete set of Volume _____
ASHE-ERIC Higher Education Reports at $144.00, over
25% off the cover price. _____

Individual reports are available for $24.00.

SHIPPING POLICY:

- Shipping (single copies only): $24.00 and under, add $5.50; to $50.00, add $6.50; to $75.00, add $7.50; to $100.00, add $9.00; to $150.00, add $10.00; orders over $150.00, call for shipping charge.
- Books are sent UPS Ground or equivalent. For faster delivery, call for charges. Alaska, Hawaii, U.S. Territories, and Foreign Countries, please call for shipping information. Order will be shipped within 24 hours after receipt of request. Orders of 10 or more books, call for shipping information. All prices shown are subject to change.
- Returns: No cash refunds—credit will be applied to future orders.

PLEASE SEND ME THE FOLLOWING REPORTS:

Quantity	Volume/No.	Title	Amount

Please check one of the following:
☐ Check enclosed, payable to GW-ERIC.
☐ Purchase order attached.
☐ Charge my credit card indicated below:
   ☐ Visa   ☐ MasterCard

Expiration Date_____

Subtotal:

Less Discount:

Total Due:

Name_____

Title _____ E-mail _____

Institution _____

Address_____

City _____ State _____ Zip_____

Phone _____ Fax _____Telex_____

Signature _____ Date_____

SEND ALL ORDERS TO:
ASHE-ERIC Higher Education Reports Series
One Dupont Cir., Ste. 630, Washington, DC 20036-1183
Phone: (202) 296-2597 ext. 13 Toll-free: (800) 773-ERIC ext. 13
FAX: (202) 452-1844
EMAIL: order@eric-he.edu
Secure on-line ordering at URL: www.eriche.org/reports

**Secure on-line ordering
is available:
visit our Web site at
www.eriche.org/reports**